2024 EDITION

BREAD MACHINE
COOKBOOK FOR BEGINNERS BIBLE

1500 DAYS OF RECIPES

STELLA BROWN

ARE YOU A BUSY MOM OR A CAREER-DRIVEN WOMAN DREAMING OF HAVING EVERYTHING UNDER CONTROL?

DO YOU WANT TO LOSE WEIGHT AND PREPARE TASTY, AFFORDABLE, AND QUICK MEALS WITHOUT LOSING YOUR MIND IN THE KITCHEN?

You find yourself running from one commitment to another, **always stressed**, and between work, family, and household duties, it feels **like there's never any time for you.**

Maybe you also want to **lose some weight**, but bland food and extreme diets are **slowly killing your soul.**

<u>You look in the mirror and feel a disconnect, as if your body doesn't reflect who you truly are inside.</u>

You try to cook healthily, but every time you find yourself grabbing something ready from the freezer or ordering takeout. You dream of preparing healthy and tasty meals that your family will love, but it feels like a Herculean task.

Have you ever wondered what your life would be like if you could eat delicious foods that also help you lose weight, without spending hours in the kitchen?

If you could find a balance between work, relationships, and self-care without constantly feeling guilty?

The solution isn't an extreme diet or another fitness app - it's a comprehensive guide that addresses the specific problems you have. A guide that speaks your language and directly addresses YOU.

Here's what you can discover with this guide:

- ✅ Unlock the simple method **to balance your work, relationships, and personal care**, and leave behind the guilt and stress;
- ✅ Discover the secrets to **balancing work, relationships, and self-care without the guilt, stress, or kitchen hassle**;
- ✅ Learn the magic of cooking techniques that allow you to savor your favorite dishes while **staying on track with your weight loss goals**
- ✅ Explore why quick-fix solutions often fail and how a blend of effective methods can lead you to real and **lasting transformation**
- ✅ Reveal the one mindset shift that can **break the cycle of failure and frustration**, paving the way for lasting success
- ✅ Learn why that time-saving meal or gym alternative might be **hindering your progress** and what you can do instead
- ✅ ...and much, much more!!

Even if your days are filled with responsibilities, you've never cooked before, or you think that healthy cooking is expensive, this book offers a fresh approach to finally attain your cooking and fitness goals.

Don't waste another moment on quick fixes and empty promises.

SCAN THE QR CODE BELOW AND BEGIN YOUR JOURNEY TOWARDS A HEALTHIER, HAPPIER, AND MORE BALANCED LIFE.

BREAD MACHINE COOKBOOK FOR BEGINNERS BIBLE
THE STEP-BY-STEP GUIDE FOR BEGINNERS TO MASTER THE ART OF BAKING. 1500 DAYS OF FRESH HOMEMADE AND STRESS-FREE RECIPES, FROM GLUTEN FREE TO WHOLE WHEAT

First Edition June 2023

© Copyright 2023 by Stella Brown - All rights reserved.

This document is geared towards providing exact and reliable information regarding the topic and issue covered. The publication is sold with the idea that the publisher is not required to render accounting, officially permitted, or otherwise qualified services. If advice is necessary, legal, or professional, a practiced individual in the profession should be ordered.

- From a Declaration of Principles, which was accepted and approved equally by a Committee of the American Bar Association and a Committee of Publishers and Associations.

In no way is it legal to reproduce, duplicate, or transmit any part of this document in either electronic means or in printed format. Recording of this publication is strictly prohibited, and any storage of this document is not allowed unless with written permission from the publisher. All rights reserved.

The information provided herein is stated to be truthful and consistent in that any liability, in terms of inattention or otherwise, by any usage or abuse of any policies, processes, or directions contained within is the solitary and utter responsibility of the recipient reader. Under no circumstances will any legal responsibility or blame be held against the publisher for any reparation, damages, or monetary loss due to the information herein, either directly or indirectly.

Respective authors own all copyrights not held by the publisher.

The information herein is offered for informational purposes solely and is universal as so. The presentation of the information is without a contract or any type of guarantee assurance.

The trademarks that are used are without any consent, and the publication of the trademark is without permission or backing by the trademark owner. All trademarks and brands within this book are for clarifying purposes only and are owned by the owners themselves, not affiliated with this document.

TABLE OF CONTENTS

INTRODUCTION — 14

CHAPTER 1
INTRODUCTION TO BREAD MACHINE — 16
1.1: BRIEF HISTORY OF BREAD MACHINES — 16
1.2: THE BENEFITS OF BREAD MACHINES AND TIPS FOR SUCCESSFUL BAKING — 18
1.3: GETTING THE RIGHT BREAD MACHINE — 19

CHAPTER 2
BREAD MACHINE BASICS — 20
2.1: ACCURATE MEASUREMENT OF INGREDIENTS — 20
2.2: PROGRAMMING THE MACHINE — 21
2.3: ESSENTIAL TECHNIQUES TO MASTER — 22
2.4: TROUBLESHOOTING COMMON PROBLEMS — 22
3.1: ADAPTING RECIPES FOR DIFFERENT TYPES OF FLOUR — 23
3.2: EFFECTIVE BREAD STORAGE METHODS — 24

CHAPTER 3
RECIPES — 26
4.1: BASIC BREAD — 27
1. EVERYDAY WHITE BREAD — 27
2. HONEY WHOLE-WHEAT BREAD — 27

3. MOLASSES WHEAT BREAD	28
4. WHOLE-WHEAT BREAD	28
5. CRUSTY FRENCH BREAD	29
6. PUMPERNICKEL BREAD	30
7. LOVELY OATMEAL BREAD	30
8. OAT BRAN MOLASSES BREAD	31
9. WHOLE-WHEAT BUTTERMILK BREAD	31
10. SOFT EGG BREAD	32
11. HEALTHY BRAN BREAD	32
12. DARK RYE BREAD	33
13. GOLDEN RAISIN BREAD	33
14. GOLDEN CORN BREAD	34
15. ENGLISH MUFFIN BREAD	34
16. TRADITIONAL ITALIAN BREAD	35
17. COCOA BREAD	35
18. GRANDMA'S CHRISTMAS BREAD	36
19. WHITE BREAD	36
20. WHITE BREAD II	37
21. RON'S BREAD MACHINE WHITE	37
22. ARGENTINIAN ROLLS	38
23. HOMEMADE SLIDER BUNS	38
24. JEWISH BREAD MACHINE CHALLAH	39
25. GREEK LOAF	39
26. HALF HOUR BREAD	40
4.2: CHEESY BREADS	**40**
1. CHEESY CHIPOTLE BREAD	40
2. ROASTED GARLIC ASIAGO BREAD	41
3. CHEDDAR CHEESE BASIL BREAD	41
4. JALAPEÑO CORN BREAD	42
5. OLIVE CHEESE BREAD	43
6. BLUE CHEESE ONION BREAD	43
7. DOUBLE CHEESE BREAD	44
8. SALAMI & MOZZARELLA BREAD	44
9. COTTAGE CHEESE BREAD (SIMPLE)	46
10. CHILE CHEESE BACON BREAD	46

11. ITALIAN PARMESAN BREAD	**47**
12. RICH CHEDDAR BREAD	**47**
13. FETA OREGANO BREAD	**48**
14. GOAT CHEESE BREAD	**48**
15. MOZZARELLA-HERB BREAD	**49**
4.3: VEGETABLE BREAD	**49**
1. YEASTED CARROT BREAD	**49**
2. SAUERKRAUT RYE BREAD	**50**
3. SAVOURY ONION BREAD	**50**
4. TOMATO HERB BREAD	**51**
5. MASHED POTATO BREAD	**51**
6. CONFETTI BREAD	**52**
7. PRETTY BORSCHT BREAD	**52**
8. YEASTED PUMPKIN BREAD	**53**
9. OATMEAL ZUCCHINI BREAD	**53**
10. HOT RED PEPPER BREAD	**54**
11. FRENCH ONION BREAD	**54**
12. GOLDEN BUTTERNUT SQUASH RAISIN BREAD	**55**
13. SWEET POTATO BREAD	**55**
14. POTATO THYME BREAD	**56**
15. CORN BREAD	**56**
4.4: KETOGENIC BREAD	**57**
1. BASIC LOW-CARB BREAD	**57**
2. ALMOND FLOUR YEAST BREAD	**57**
3. ALMOND MILK BREAD	**58**
4. FLAXSEED BREAD	**58**
5. ALMOND FLOUR BREAD	**59**
6. SANDWICH BREAD	**59**
7. MACADAMIA BREAD	**60**
8. TOASTING BREAD	**60**
9. MEDITERRANEAN BREAD	**61**
10. ITALIAN ALPERITO BREAD	**61**
11. KETO BAGUETTE	**62**
12. KETO BRIOCHE BREAD	**62**

13. OREGANO ONION FOCACCIA	63
14. KETO FOCACCIA	64
15. ZUCCHINI CIABATTA	64

4.5: SOURDOUGH BREAD — 66

1. SIMPLE SOURDOUGH STARTER (NO-YEAST WHOLE WHEAT SOURDOUGH STARTER)	66
2. BASIC SOURDOUGH BREAD	67
3. WHOLE-WHEAT SOURDOUGH BREAD	67
4. MULTIGRAIN SOURDOUGH BREAD	68
5. FAUX SOURDOUGH BREAD	68
6. SOURDOUGH MILK BREAD	69
7. LEMON SOURDOUGH BREAD	69
8. SAN FRANCISCO SOURDOUGH BREAD	70
9. SOURDOUGH BEER BREAD	70
10. CRUSTY SOURDOUGH BREAD	71
11. SOURDOUGH CHEDDAR BREAD	71
12. HERB SOURDOUGH	72
13. CRANBERRY PECAN SOURDOUGH	72
14. DARK CHOCOLATE SOURDOUGH	73

4.6: FRUIT BREAD — 73

1. PINEAPPLE COCONUT BREAD	73
2. BLACK OLIVE BREAD	74
3. WARM SPICED PUMPKIN BREAD	75
4. ROBUST DATE BREAD	75
5. APPLE SPICE BREAD	76
6. LEMON-LIME BLUEBERRY BREAD	76
7. BANANA WHOLE-WHEAT BREAD	77
8. ORANGE CRANBERRY BREAD	77
9. PLUM ORANGE BREAD	78
10. PEACHES & CREAM BREAD	78
11. FRESH BLUEBERRY BREAD	79
12. BLUEBERRY OATMEAL BREAD	79
13. FRAGRANT ORANGE BREAD	80
14. MOIST OATMEAL APPLE BREAD	80
15. STRAWBERRY SHORTCAKE BREAD	81

4.7: GRAIN, SEED, AND NUT BREADS — 81

1. WHOLE-WHEAT SEED BREAD	81
2. MULTIGRAIN BREAD	82
3. TOASTED PECAN BREAD	82
4. MARKET SEED BREAD	83
5. CRACKED WHEAT BREAD	83
6. DOUBLE COCONUT BREAD	84
7. HONEYED BULGUR BREAD	84
8. FLAXSEED HONEY BREAD	85
9. CHIA SESAME BREAD	85
10. QUINOA WHOLE WHEAT BREAD	86
11. PEANUT BUTTER BREAD	86
12. TOASTED HAZELNUT BREAD	87
13. OATMEAL SEED BREAD	87
14. NUTTY WHEAT BREAD	88
15. SUNFLOWER BREAD	88
16. RAISIN SEED BREAD	89
17. QUINOA OATMEAL BREAD	89

4.8: HERB AND SPICE BREADS — 90

1. OATMEAL-SUNFLOWER BREAD RECIPE	90
2. BREAD MACHINE - BACON BREAD	91
3. BREAD MACHINE LEMON BREAD RECIPE	92
4. BREAD MACHINE PIZZA DOUGH WITH VARIATIONS	93
5. ROASTED GARLIC BREAD FOR THE BREAD MACHINE	93
6. BREAD MACHINE GARLIC BASIL BREAD	94
7. PEPPER ASIAGO LOAF	94
8. SPICED RAISIN BREAD	95
9. MEXICAN BREAD	95
10. BREAD MACHINE HERB & PARMESAN BREAD RECIPE	96
11. ITALIAN HERB BREAD	96
12. PEPPERONI BREAD	97
13. SPAGHETTI BREAD	97
14. MULTIGRAIN SPECIAL BREAD	98
15. CRACKED PEPPER BREAD	98
16. CARAWAY DILL BREAD	99

4.9: INTERNATIONAL BREADS — 99
1. ITALIAN PANETTONE — 99
2. ITALIAN POP BREAD — 100
3. BREAD OF THE DEAD (PAN DE MUERTOS) — 100
4. MEXICAN SWEET BREAD — 101
5. CHALLAH — 101
6. RUSSIAN BLACK BREAD — 102
7. RUSSIAN RYE BREAD — 102
8. PORTUGUESE CORN BREAD — 103
9. AMISH WHEAT BREAD — 103
10. BRITISH HOT CROSS BUNS — 104
11. HAWAIIAN BREAD — 104
12. GREEK EASTER BREAD — 105
13. FIJI SWEET POTATO BREAD — 105
14. ZA'ATAR BREAD — 106

4.10: SWEET BREADS — 106
1. CHOCOLATE CHIP PEANUT BUTTER BANANA BREAD — 106
2. CHOCOLATE SOUR CREAM BREAD — 107
3. NECTARINE COBBLER BREAD — 107
4. SOUR CREAM MAPLE BREAD — 108
5. BARMBRACK BREAD — 108
6. APPLE BUTTER BREAD — 109
7. CRUSTY HONEY BREAD — 109
8. HONEY GRANOLA BREAD — 110
9. BLACK BREAD — 110
10. APPLE CIDER BREAD — 111
11. COFFEE CAKE — 111
12. PUMPKIN COCONUT BREAD — 112
13. VANILLA ALMOND MILK BREAD — 112
14. TRIPLE CHOCOLATE BREAD — 113
15. CHOCOLATE OATMEAL BANANA BREAD — 113

4.11: HOLIDAY BREADS — 114
1. PANETTONE BREAD — 114
2. WHITE CHOCOLATE CRANBERRY BREAD — 115

3. EGGNOG BREAD	**115**
4. WHOLE-WHEAT CHALLAH	**116**
5. PORTUGUESE SWEET BREAD	**116**
6. PECAN MAPLE BREAD	**117**
7. NANA'S GINGERBREAD	**117**
8. BREAD MACHINE BRIOCHE	**118**
9. TRADITIONAL PASCHA	**118**
10. RAISIN & NUT PASKA	**119**
11. HONEY CAKE	**119**
12. CHRISTMAS FRUIT BREAD	**120**
13. STOLLEN BREAD	**120**
14. JULEKAKE	**121**
15. SPIKED EGGNOG BREAD	**121**
16. HOT BUTTERED RUM BREAD	**122**

4.12: GLUTEN-FREE BREADS — 122

1. GLUTEN-FREE WHITE BREAD	**122**
2. BROWN RICE BREAD	**123**
3. BROWN RICE & CRANBERRY BREAD	**123**
4. GLUTEN-FREE PEASANT BREAD	**124**
5. GLUTEN-FREE HAWAIIAN LOAF	**124**
6. VEGAN GLUTEN-FREE BREAD	**125**

4.13: CREATIVE COMBINATION BREAD — 125

1. ZUCCHINI PECAN BREAD	**125**
2. RAISIN BRAN BREAD	**126**
3. LEMON POPPY SEED BREAD	**126**
4. MUSTARD RYE BREAD	**127**
5. HAM & CHEESE BREAD	**127**
6. SAUSAGE HERB BREAD	**128**
7. WILD RICE HAZELNUT BREAD	**128**
8. SPINACH FETA BREAD	**129**
9. RUM RAISIN BREAD	**129**
10. BACON CORN BREAD	**130**
11. OATMEAL COFFEE BREAD	**130**
12. CHERRY PISTACHIO BREAD	**131**

13. BANANA COCONUT BREAD	**131**
14. EASY HONEY BEER BREAD	**132**
15. COFFEE MOLASSES BREAD	**132**
16. CHERRY ALMOND BREAD	**133**

CHAPTER 4
GLOSSARY AND RESOURCES   134
5.1: GLOSSARY   134
5.2: RESOURCES   136

CONCLUSION   137

INDEX OF RECIPES   139

BREAD MACHINE COOKBOOK FOR BEGINNERS BIBLE

THE STEP-BY-STEP GUIDE FOR BEGINNERS TO MASTER THE ART OF BAKING. 1500 DAYS OF FRESH HOMEMADE AND STRESS-FREE RECIPES, FROM GLUTEN FREE TO WHOLE WHEAT

STELLA BROWN

INTRODUCTION

Welcome to The Easy Bread Machine Cookbook: Foolproof Recipes for Stress-Free Baking. Whether you're an apprentice or a qualified bread maker, this book is suggested to be your complete handbook for making delicious homemade bread using a bread machine.

Baking bread from scratch can be intimidating, but with the help of a bread machine, it becomes an enjoyable and hassle-free experience. This cookbook is specifically tailored for beginners who want to explore the art of bread making or for those who seek the convenience and simplicity offered by a bread machine. With step-by-step instructions, helpful tips, and a wide variety of delectable recipes, you'll soon be savoring the mouth-watering aroma and spongy goodness of freshly baked bread right in your own kitchen.

The Easy Bread Machine Cookbook starts by providing an introduction to bread machines, offering a comprehensive overview of their functionality and the different types available in the market. You'll gain valuable insights into selecting the right bread machine that suits your needs and preferences. Common misconceptions and frequently asked questions will also be addressed to ensure you have a solid foundation before diving into the world of bread making.

The book then dives into the essential "Bread Machine Basics" to equip you with the necessary skills and techniques for operating your bread machine with confidence. You'll learn how to measure ingredients accurately, program your machine for different bread cycles, and troubleshoot common problems that may arise during the baking process. From understanding the various cycles to utilizing different techniques, this section will empower you to make the most out of your bread machine.

In order to help you achieve the exact loaf of bread every single time, the "Tips and Tricks" section provides invaluable advice. You'll discover how to adjust recipes to accommodate different types of flour, master the art of bread storage for optimal freshness, and troubleshoot common issues that may occur along the way. These tips and tricks will elevate your bread making skills, ensuring consistently impressive results.

The book also includes a comprehensive glossary of baking terms and a list of resources for further reading and learning. This will serve as your go-to reference, expanding your knowledge of bread making and allowing you to explore new techniques and recipes beyond the scope of this book.

Finally, the heart of The Easy Bread Machine Cookbook lies in its collection of 201 easy-to-follow recipes. From classic white bread to hearty wheat bread, savoury herb-infused loaves, to gluten-free options, you'll find a wide selection of bread methods to suit every palate and dietary preference. Each recipe provides detailed instructions, ingredient lists, and nutritional values, ensuring that you have all the information you need to create delectable loaves of bread.

Throughout the book, the ingredients are listed clearly, and the directions are easy to follow. Helpful tips and variations are included to encourage experimentation and cater to different tastes and preferences. Where possible, vibrant photographs are provided to guide you visually through the bread making process, inspiring you to create beautiful and delicious bread right at home.

The Easy Bread Machine Cookbook is your companion on a journey of bread making adventure. Whether you're seeking the joy of baking from scratch or the convenience of using a bread machine, this book will empower you to create mouth-watering loaves of bread that will impress your family and friends. So, grab your bread machine, unleash your inner baker, and get ready to experience the satisfaction and delight of homemade bread. Let's embark on this delicious journey together.

CHAPTER 1
INTRODUCTION TO BREAD MACHINE

1.1: BRIEF HISTORY OF BREAD MACHINES

Throughout the late 1980s and early 1990s, a ground-breaking invention emerged that would revolutionize the way people made bread at home—the bread machine. These innovative devices were designed with the purpose of simplifying and streamlining the bread making process, making it accessible to anyone. In their early stages, bread machines were relatively basic, featuring a simple timer that allowed users to program the start and end of the baking cycle. However, as time went on, these machines underwent significant advancements and became more sophisticated, offering a range of features and capabilities.

The initial models of bread machines paved the way for future developments in the field. With time, manufacturers recognized the growing demand and sought to incorporate additional capabilities into their products. One of the most notable advancements was the ability of bread machines to bake different types of bread, catering to a variety of dietary preferences and requirements. Whether individuals desired gluten-free options or whole-grain varieties, the bread machine offered the flexibility to accommodate these needs. Furthermore, users gained the ability to select the crust colour of their bread, allowing for a customized baking experience.

As the popularity of bread machines soared, manufacturers began to create models that catered to specific household needs. Families and larger households could choose machines with larger loaf capacities, ensuring an ample supply of fresh bread. On the other hand, those with smaller kitchens or limited counter space could opt for compact machines designed to fit their needs. Some bread machines even featured built-in storage compartments, providing a convenient solution for keeping utensils and ingredients within reach during the baking process.

Recent years have witnessed further advancements in bread machine technology, with the integration of cutting-edge features. Voice control, Wi-Fi connectivity, and smartphone app integration have become key selling points for modern bread machines. These advancements allow users to control their machines remotely, providing the convenience of initiating the baking process from anywhere. With the ability to program specific baking periods, users can ensure that their favourite type of bread, such as garlic bread, is readily available whenever desired.

While bread machines have undoubtedly transformed home bread baking, they are not without their challenges. Some users have reported that the bread produced by these machines tends to be denser and heavier compared to traditionally baked bread. Achieving the desired level of crust crispness can also pose a challenge. In addition, certain individuals have found the machines to be noisy and somewhat difficult to clean.

Nonetheless, the popularity of bread machines remains steadfast among individuals who seek the convenience and efficiency they offer. The ability to effortlessly produce fresh bread at home without constant monitoring is a significant advantage. A bread machine can be an invaluable addition to your kitchen arsenal.

The history of bread machines is a testament to continuous innovation and evolution. From their humble beginnings as timer-controlled devices, they have evolved into sophisticated appliances with a multitude of features and benefits. Today, bread machines cater to the diverse needs of individuals who enjoy baking their own bread at home. Whether you are seeking a quick and easy solution or advanced tools to achieve the perfect loaf, a bread machine provides a convenient and effective means of bread baking.

1.2: THE BENEFITS OF BREAD MACHINES AND TIPS FOR SUCCESSFUL BAKING

Bread machines have brought about a revolution in home bread baking, offering a multitude of benefits that have made the process more convenient and accessible to all. The key advantage lies in the simplicity they provide, streamlining the entire bread making process. Users can effortlessly add their ingredients, select the desired settings, and let the machine take care of the rest. This not only saves precious time and effort but also ensures consistent and perfectly baked bread as the end result. The versatility of bread machines is another noteworthy aspect, as they can accommodate various types of bread, including gluten-free and whole-grain options, catering to the diverse dietary needs of individuals. By offering control over the ingredients used, bread machines empower users to make healthier choices, promoting long-term well-being and cost-effectiveness when compared to store-bought bread. Cleaning is also hassle-free, thanks to the presence of removable parts that are dishwasher safe.

When it comes to the key ingredients for successful bread baking, precision in measurement is of utmost importance. Flour, yeast, salt, sweetener, and liquid play vital roles in achieving the desired outcome. The choice of flour, whether it be bread flour, all-purpose flour, whole wheat flour, or gluten-free flour, significantly impacts the final texture and structure of the bread. Yeast, on the other hand, acts as the catalyst for proper rising, while the amount of salt, sweetener, and fat can be adjusted according to personal taste preferences. Liquid, such as water, milk, or juice, not only adds moisture to the dough but also activates the yeast for optimal fermentation. In terms of equipment, a bread machine is a primary requirement for successful bread baking at home. Additionally, measuring cups and spoons ensure accurate ingredient measurement, a bread pan is essential for shaping the dough, a kneading blade aids in mixing and kneading, and a timer allows for precise timing.

To achieve the best possible results when utilizing a bread machine, precise measurement of ingredients becomes paramount. It is crucial to employ high-quality components such as unbleached flour and active dry yeast to elevate the overall taste and texture of the bread. Different types of flour yield distinct textures, with bread flour imparting a chewier consistency and all-purpose flour yielding a softer and more tender crumb. Paying attention to the temperature of the liquid utilized is equally vital. Optimal yeast activation is achieved by employing warm liquids within the temperature range of 38°C to 43°C (100°F to 110°F). This temperature range fosters effective yeast fermentation, leading to proper rising and development of flavours in the bread. Adhering to the recommended order of ingredient addition, as specified in the bread machine's instructions, is also crucial. Typically, this involves adding the liquid first, followed by the dry ingredients, and finally incorporating the yeast. By following this sequence, optimal mixing and even distribution of ingredients are ensured, resulting in a well-balanced and uniformly textured loaf of bread.

In conclusion, bread machines have transformed the landscape of home bread baking, offering unparalleled convenience and a host of benefits. With their ability to simplify the process, accommodate various types of bread, and provide control over ingredients, bread machines have become an indispensable tool for bread enthusiasts of all skill levels. By carefully selecting high-quality ingredients, adhering to precise measurements, and following the recommended ingredient order, individuals can achieve outstanding results and savour the joy of newly baked bread in the comfort of their homes.

1.3: GETTING THE RIGHT BREAD MACHINE

When faced with the wide array of bread machine options available, selecting the most suitable one can feel overwhelming. To help in the decision-making procedure, here are a few factors to consider:

1. Capacity: Bread machines are available in various sizes. Consider your household size and typical bread consumption. For smaller families, a machine capable of making 1 to 1.5-pound loaves should suffice, while larger families may require a machine that produces 2 to 2.5-pound loaves.
2. Versatility: Assess the types of bread and additional features you desire. If you wish to explore beyond basic bread, seek a machine that can handle different dough types, including whole grain, gluten-free, and doughs for pastries or pizzas.
3. Ease of Use: Evaluate the user-friendliness of the machine. Look for clear controls, a readable display, and a well-written, comprehensive user manual. Additionally, consider the convenience of removing and cleaning the bread pan.
4. Budget: Bread machine prices vary significantly. Keep in mind that these machines may lack durability or versatility. On the other hand, the most expensive models may offer unnecessary fancy features. Assess your needs and set a budget that aligns with them.

The true value of a bread machine lies in its convenience and versatility. It serves as a valuable investment for bread enthusiasts who desire the delightful taste of homemade bread without the time-consuming effort of kneading dough and closely monitoring its progress.

Choosing the appropriate bread machine which ultimately depends on individual requirements and preferences. By understanding the operational aspects and key features offered by these machines, you can identify the model that best complements your lifestyle, allowing you to relish the pleasure of freshly baked bread at your convenience.

CHAPTER 2
BREAD MACHINE BASICS

Creating homemade bread from scratch can be a daunting endeavour. However, a bread machine simplifies and streamlines this process, making it much more manageable. With a bread machine, you can effortlessly enjoy fresh, homemade bread. Let's explore a step-by-step guide to mastering the basics of using a bread machine.

2.1: ACCURATE MEASUREMENT OF INGREDIENTS

Achieving precision in ingredient measurement is crucial for successful baking. Even slight deviations can lead to significant variations in the final outcome. Let's delve into the proper techniques for measuring ingredients accurately:

Flour

When measuring flour, employ the "spoon and sweep" technique. Spoon the flour into the determining cup, then level the excess with a knife. Avoid packing down or tapping the cup, as this can result in an excessive amount of flour.

Liquid Ingredients

For measuring liquid ingredients such as water, milk, or oil, use a clear, graduated measuring cup. Ensure that you observe the cup at eye level to obtain accurate measurements.

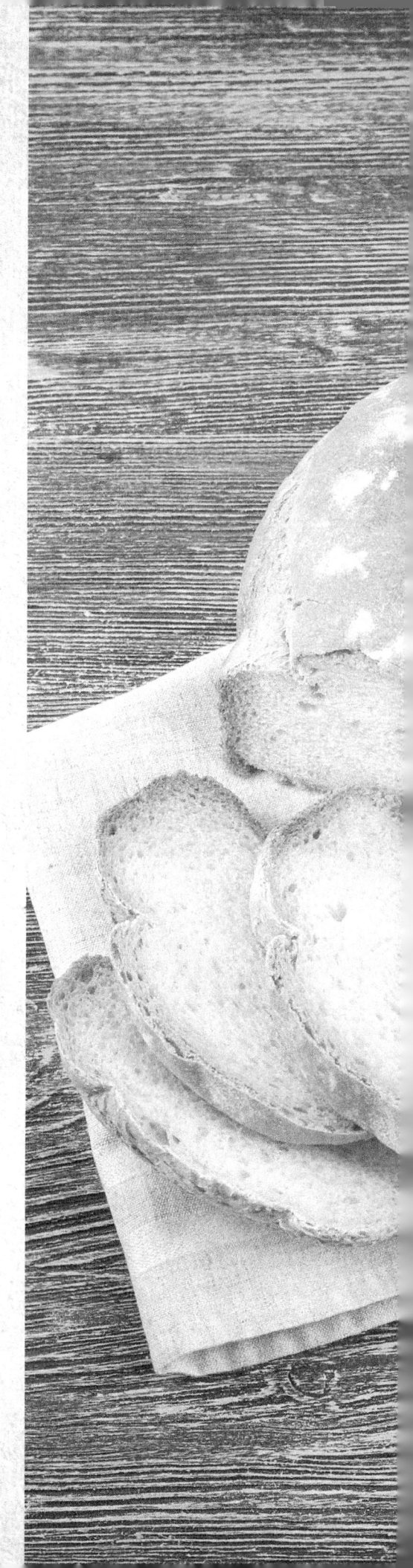

Yeast

When measuring small quantities of yeast, employ a measuring spoon for precise results. Level it with a knife for exactness.

Salt and Sugar

Similar to yeast, use a measuring spoon for salt and sugar, as they play vital roles in yeast fermentation and bread flavour.

2.2: PROGRAMMING THE MACHINE

Most bread machines are equipped with pre-programmed settings designed for specific bread types. Let's explore these settings:

Basic or White Cycle

This standard set is suitable for making various types of bread, especially white bread. It involves kneading the dough, allowing it to rise, and finally baking it.

Whole Wheat Cycle

Specifically tailored for recipes utilizing substantial amounts of whole wheat flour, this cycle incorporates longer rise times to accommodate the denser and heavier dough.

Dough Cycle

The dough cycle preparations the dough without baking it, making it ideal for recipes where the dough needs to be shaped by hand, risen, and then baked in a conventional oven.

Gluten-Free Cycle

As this is designed specifically for baking gluten-free bread, the cycle features modified kneading and rising phases to cater to the unique requirements of gluten-free recipes.

Quick Bread Cycle

This cycle is intended for bread that does not require yeast, such as banana or zucchini bread.

To program your bread machine, simply select the appropriate cycle for your recipe and initiate the process by pressing the start button. If your machine offers options for crust colour and loaf size, make sure to set them accordingly.

2.3: ESSENTIAL TECHNIQUES TO MASTER

Here are some crucial techniques to become adept at when using a bread machine:

Adding Ingredients

Always follow the order suggested by your bread machine manual when adding ingredients. Typically, liquids are added first, followed by dry ingredients, with yeast added last.

Checking Dough Consistency

Around 10 minutes into the kneading cycle, examine the dough's consistency. It should form a smooth, round ball. If the dough is too dry, gradually add a tablespoon of liquid until it reaches the desired consistency. Conversely, if it's too wet, incorporate a tablespoon of flour at a time until the ideal consistency is achieved.

Utilizing the Delay Timer

Many bread machines are equipped with a delay timer feature, enabling you to add ingredients and program the machine to start at a later time. This is particularly useful for waking up to the odour of freshly baked daily bread.

By following these steps, employing accurate ingredient measurement techniques, and mastering essential bread machine techniques, you can embark on a successful journey of creating delicious homemade bread with ease.

2.4: TROUBLESHOOTING COMMON PROBLEMS

Despite your best efforts, you may encounter occasional challenges when using your bread machine. Here are some ordinary troubles that may arise and their corresponding solutions:

Bread Collapses During Baking

If you find that your bread collapses during the baking process, it is often an indication of excessive yeast or liquid in the recipe. To rectify this, reduce the amounts of yeast and liquid slightly in your next batch. This adjustment should help maintain the proper structure and prevent the bread from collapsing.

Bread is Too Dense

If your bread turns out overly dense, it could be a result of insufficient liquid, excessive flour, or insufficient yeast. To address this issue, you can make a few adjustments. Firstly, try increasing the amount of liquid in the recipe to provide more moisture and promote a lighter texture. Secondly, consider reducing the amount of flour used to prevent an overly dense consistency. Lastly, ensure that you are using an adequate amount of yeast to facilitate proper rising and fermentation.

Bread is undercooked

If you find that your bread is consistently undercooked, there could be a couple of factors at play. Firstly, it is possible that the loaf size is too large for your bread machine. In such cases, opting for a smaller loaf size can allow for more thorough and even baking. Additionally, check the wattage of your machine, as a lower wattage may require an extended baking time to ensure proper doneness.

In summary, utilizing a bread machine requires precise ingredient measurements, a solid understanding of various machine cycles, and the capacity to address common challenges that may arise. By attaining mastery of these essential elements, you can confidently embark on your bread making adventure and savour the delicious outcome of freshly baked bread made at home.

Chapter 3

Tips and Tricks

In addition to the essential techniques covered in the previous chapters, this section will delve into a range of valuable tips and tricks to help you achieve the perfect loaf of bread every time. These insights will include adjusting recipes for various types of flour, effective bread storage methods, and troubleshooting common problems that may arise during the bread making process. By incorporating these expert recommendations into your breadmaking routine, you can elevate your skills and enjoy consistently excellent results.

3.1: ADAPTING RECIPES FOR DIFFERENT TYPES OF FLOUR

Different types of flour can significantly impact the texture, flavour, and overall outcome of your bread. Understanding how to adjust recipes for specific flours will allow you to tailor your bread to your preferences. Consider the following guidelines:

1. All-Purpose Flour: This versatile flour is commonly used in bread making. It produces a balanced

texture and flavour. For recipes that call for other types of flour, you can typically substitute all-purpose flour with satisfying results.
2. Bread Flour: Bread flour has an elevated protein satisfied, resulting in a more elastic and chewy texture. When using bread flour, you may need to adjust the liquid content slightly, as it absorbs more moisture than other flours.
3. Whole Wheat Flour: Whole wheat flour adds a rich, nutty flavour and denser texture to the bread. Since whole wheat flour grips more liquid, you may need to increase the liquid measurements in your recipe to maintain the desired consistency.
4. Gluten-Free Flour: Gluten-free flour blends are formulated to mimic the texture and structure of traditional wheat-based flour. It is crucial to follow recipes specifically designed for gluten-free baking, as these flours require different ratios of liquid, binding agents, and rising agents.

So, experimenting with different flours and adjusting recipes will allow you to discover unique combinations and create bread that perfectly suits your taste preferences.

3.2: EFFECTIVE BREAD STORAGE METHODS

Here are some tips to help you store your homemade bread properly and maintain its freshness and quality:

Allow bread to cool: Once you remove your bread from the machine, let it cool completely on a wire rack. This step prevents condensation and helps maintain a crisp crust.

Use airtight containers: After the bread has cooled, keep it in a sealed container or a resealable plastic bag. This helps retain moisture and prevents the bread from drying out.

Room temperature storage: If you plan to consume the bread within a few days, storing it at room temperature is acceptable. However, note that it may lose some freshness and become stale more quickly compared to refrigerated storage.

Refrigeration: In warmer climates or during humid seasons, refrigerating your bread can extend its freshness, especially for longer-term storage. Before refrigerating, wrap the bread securely in plastic wrap or position it in a resealable bag.

Freezing: Freezing is an excellent option for preserving bread for an extended period. Slice the bread before freezing and wrap individual slices or the entire loaf tightly in plastic wrap. Then, place them in a freezer-safe bag. Thaw frozen bread at room temperature or gently reheat it in an oven or toaster.

By following these storage methods, you can enjoy your homemade bread at its best, preserving its texture, flavour, and quality over time.

3.3: Solving Common Issues

Even with proper techniques, occasional challenges may arise during the breadmaking process. Here are solutions to common problems:

1. Bread Not Rising: If your bread fails to rise adequately, check the freshness of your yeast, ensure

proper kneading and rising times, and verify that your ingredients are at the correct temperature. Increasing the yeast amount or adding a pinch of sugar to activate the yeast can also help.
2. Dense Texture: A dense texture may be caused by using too much flour, insufficient liquid, or insufficient kneading. Adjust your measurements, ensuring a proper balance of ingredients, and knead the dough thoroughly to achieve a lighter texture.
3. Crumbly Texture: A crumbly texture could indicate insufficient moisture or over-baking. Check the liquid measurements and reduce the baking time slightly to prevent excessive dryness.
4. Uneven Browning: Uneven browning may result from improper positioning in the bread machine or variations in the machine's heating elements. Ensure the dough is evenly distributed in the pan and consider rotating the pan during baking.
5. Sinking in the Middle: Bread sinking in the middle may be due to excessive liquid or improper rising times. Adjust the liquid measurements and ensure sufficient rising time for the dough to achieve proper structure.

By understanding these troubleshooting techniques, you can overcome common challenges and fine-tune your breadmaking process for consistently exceptional results.

In conclusion, by implementing the tips and tricks outlined in this chapter, you can enhance your breadmaking skills and create remarkable loaves of bread every time. Whether it involves adjusting recipes for different types of flour, employing effective bread storage methods, or troubleshooting common issues, these expert recommendations will empower you to elevate your breadmaking journey and delight in the satisfaction of homemade bread that surpasses your expectations.

CHAPTER 3
RECIPES

4.1: Basic Bread

1. EVERYDAY WHITE BREAD

Preparation Time: 20 minutes **Cooking Time:** 2 hours **Servings:** 2

INGREDIENTS

- All Purpose flour, 3 + 3/4 cups
- Butter, 3 tbsp
- Lukewarm Water, 1 cup.
- Yeast (Bread machine), 2 tsp
- Lukewarm milk, 1/3 cup
- Sugar, 3 tbsp
- Salt, 1 tsp

DIRECTIONS

1. Put all of the ingredients in the bread machine.
2. Choose a two-pound loaf with a medium crust as the default option. Choose "start."
3. After baking, allow it to cool completely before slicing.

Nutritional Value: 75 Kcal, Protein: 2g, Carb: 3g, Fat: 4g,
Note: Enjoy this classic white bread as a versatile staple for sandwiches or toast.

2. HONEY WHOLE-WHEAT BREAD

Preparation Time: 5 minutes **Cooking Time:** 3 hours 25 minutes **Servings:** 3

INGREDIENTS

- Olive oil, 1/3 cup
- Flour (whole wheat), 4 1/2 cups
- Honey, 1/3 cup
- warm water, 1 1/2 cups
- Yeast, 1 tbsp
- Gluten, 1 tsp
- Kosher salt, 2 tsp

DIRECTIONS

1. Put water, honey & oil in the machine. Then put salt, half flour, leftover flour & gluten.
2. In the middle, make a well and add the yeast.
3. Pick whole wheat bread with a thin crust.
4. Serve warm bread.

Nutritional Value: 84 Kcal, Protein: 3g, Carb: 5g, Fat: 2g
Note: This wholesome bread is made with whole wheat flour and honey for a touch of natural sweetness.

3. MOLASSES WHEAT BREAD

Preparation Time: 10 minutes **Cooking Time:** 4 hours **Servings:** 3

INGREDIENTS

- Water, 3/4 cup
- Whole wheat flour, 1 + 3/4 cup
- Melted butter, 3 tbsp.
- Milk, 1/3 cup
- Molasses, 3 tbsp
- Sugar, 2 tbsp
- Yeast (Fast-rising), 2 + 1/4 tsp
- Bread flour, 2 cups
- Salt, 1 tsp

DIRECTIONS

1. In the machine, Put all ingredients as per the recommended machine's order.
2. Ensure that the ingredients stay at room temperature.
3. Select a basic setting with a light crust.
4. Eat while it's fresh.

Nutritional Value: 80 Kcal, Protein: 1g, Carb: 4g, Fat: 9g,
Note: The addition of molasses gives this bread a rich and slightly sweet flavor.

4. WHOLE-WHEAT BREAD

Preparation Time: 10 minutes **Cooking Time:** 4 hours **Servings:** 2

INGREDIENTS

- whole wheat flour, 3 + 1/3 cup
- water, 1½ cup
- Powdered milk, 2 tbsp
- Honey, 2 tbsp
- Molasses, 2 tbsp
- Salt: 1½ tsp
- Margarine, 2 tbsp
- Yeast, 1½ tsp

DIRECTIONS

1. Put liquid ingredients first, then dry ingredients according to the sequence specified by your machine.
2. Combine water & milk powder. Add to the bread machine after heating in the microwave for thirty seconds.
3. Choose a 2 lb. loaf & start the whole wheat bread process.
4. Serve while it's fresh.

Nutritional Value: 114 Kcal, Protein: 5g, Carb: 9g, Fat: 6g,
Note: With the goodness of whole wheat flour, this bread is a healthier alternative to white bread.

5. CRUSTY FRENCH BREAD

Preparation Time: 10 minutes   **Cooking Time:** 3 hours   **Servings:** 1

INGREDIENTS

- Instant yeast, 1 tsp
- Sugar, 1½ tsp
- Salt, 1½ tsp
- Lukewarm Water, 1 cup
- Butter, 1½ tsp
- Bread flour, 3 cups
- **For Glaze:**
- Water, 1 tsp
- Egg white, 1

DIRECTIONS

1. In the bread machine, put all of the ingredients according to the recommended order.
2. Choosing the dough cycle. After Five to ten minutes, manage the dough's texture by mixing in flour (1 tbsp) if it's too moist. Add 1 tbsp of water if it's excessively dry. It must stick to the edges and then pull away.
3. Take the dough out of your machine & place it on a freshly floured table. Create loaves in the form of cylinders. Create French bread shapes.
4. The loaves should be put in greased baking pans. It should rise in the hot area while being covered with a cloth.
5. Let the oven warm up to 425 degrees. Water and egg are combined to form the glaze. Apply a glaze to the loaf's surface. On the dough's surface, make incisions. For twenty minutes, cook in the oven.
6. Reduce the oven's heat to 350 F and bake for a further five to ten minutes till it's golden brown.
7. Assess the interior temperature of the bread. It ought to be 195 F. Cool a little bit and serve while it's fresh

Nutritional Value: 130 Kcal, Protein: 2g, Carb: 3g, Fat: 4g
Note: Enjoy the crispy crust and soft interior of this classic French bread.

6. PUMPERNICKEL BREAD

Preparation Time: 10 minutes **Cooking Time:** 3 hours 20 minutes **Servings:** 3

INGREDIENTS

- Vegetable oil, 1½ tbsp
- Warm water, 1⅛ cups
- Cocoa, 3 tbsp
- Molasses, ⅓ cup
- bread flour, 1⅛ cups
- Caraway seed, 1 tbsp
- Salt, 1½ tsp
- Bread machine yeast, 2 1/2 tsp
- Whole wheat flour, 1 cup
- Rye flour, 1 cup
- Wheat gluten, 1½ tbsp

DIRECTIONS

1. in the bread machine, put all ingredients & choose the default cycle, then select start.
2. Serve while it's fresh.

Nutritional Value: 100 Kcal, Protein: 12g, Carb: 13g, Fat: 14g
Note: Made with rye flour and cocoa, this bread has a distinctive dark color and robust flavor.

7. LOVELY OATMEAL BREAD

Preparation Time: 10 minutes **Cooking Time:** 3 hours **Servings:** 1

INGREDIENTS

- Unsalted Butter(sliced), 3 Tbsp
- Lukewarm milk, 1 cup
- Bread Machine Yeast, 1½ Tsp
- Old Fashioned Oatmeal, 3/4 Cup
- Bread Flour, 2 ¼ cups
- Salt, 1½ tsp
- Brown Sugar, 1 tbsp for non-sweet & 1/4 Cup for sweet

DIRECTIONS

1. In the order, put all the ingredients into the bread machine.
2. Pick up a 1.5 lb. loaf. Light setting & thin crust. Start by pressing the button.
3. Sprinkle Oatmeal to a top layer as the baking cycle starts.
4. Serve while it's fresh.

Nutritional Value: 110 Kcal, Protein: 8g, Carb: 1g, Fat: 4g
Note: The addition of oats adds texture and a hint of nuttiness to this delightful bread.

8. OAT BRAN MOLASSES BREAD

Preparation Time: 10 minutes **Cooking Time:** 3 hours **Servings:** 1

INGREDIENTS

- Flour (Whole wheat), 3 cups
- Molasses, 1/4 cup
- Warm water, 1 cup
- Yeast, 2 ¼ tsp
- Salt, ½ tsp
- Melted margarine, 2 tbsp
- Oat bran, 1 cup

DIRECTIONS

1. In the order, put all the ingredients into the bread machine.
2. Pick up a 1. lb. loaf, Whole wheat. Start by pressing the button.

Nutritional Value: 120 Kcal, Protein: 7g, Carb: 12g, Fat: 17g
Note: This bread is packed with fiber and flavor, thanks to the combination of oat bran and molasses.

9. WHOLE-WHEAT BUTTERMILK BREAD

Preparation Time: 10 minutes **Cooking Time:** 3 hours **Servings:** 2

INGREDIENTS

- Whole wheat flour, 2 cups
- Bread flour, 2 cups
- Salt, 1 3/4 tsp
- Olive oil, 2 tbsp
- Water, 6 tbsp
- Buttermilk, 1 cup
- Caraway seeds, 1 ½ tsp
- Sugar, 3 tbsp
- Celery seeds, 1 ½ tsp
- Yeast (Bread machine), 2 tsp
- Mustard seeds, ½ tsp
- Sesame seeds, 1 ½ tsp

DIRECTIONS

1. In the order, put all the ingredients into the bread machine.
2. After forming a well, sprinkle the yeast on top.
3. Choose the basic cycle with a light crust. Click "Start"
4. Serve while it's fresh.

Nutritional Value: 140 Kcal, Protein: 18g, Carb: 16g, Fat: 9g
Note: Buttermilk lends a tender texture to this whole wheat bread, perfect for sandwiches or toast.

10. SOFT EGG BREAD

Preparation Time: 10 minutes   **Cooking Time:** 2 hours   **Servings:** 3

INGREDIENTS

- Bread flour (Bread machine), 3 cups
- Butter (Softened), 2 tbsp
- Milk, 2/3 cup
- Bread machine yeast, 2 tsp
- Sugar, 2 tbsp
- Eggs, 2
- Salt, 1 tsp

DIRECTIONS

1. In the order, put all the ingredients into the bread machine.
2. Choose the basic cycle with a light crust. Click "Start"
3. Serve while it's fresh.

Nutritional Value: 110 Kcal, Protein: 6g, Carb: 3g, Fat: 5g
Note: Enjoy the soft and fluffy texture of this bread, made with the richness of eggs.

11. HEALTHY BRAN BREAD

Preparation Time: 5 minutes   **Cooking Time:** 3 hours 40 minutes   **Servings:** 4

INGREDIENTS

- A beaten egg and one cup of water combined.
- Kosher salt, 1½ tsp
- Honey, 1 tbsp
- Olive oil, 1 tbsp
- Yeast (bread machine), ½ tsp
- Wheat bran (unprocessed), 5½ Tbsp
- Bread flour, 3 cups

DIRECTIONS

1. In the order, put all the ingredients into the bread machine.
2. If necessary, add extra flour or water to change the dough's form.
3. Choose the basic cycle and hit the start button.
4. Serve while it's fresh.

Nutritional Value: 95 Kcal, Protein: 8g, Carb: 3g, Fat: 16g
Note: Packed with wheat bran, this bread is a great choice for a fiber-rich breakfast or snack.

12. DARK RYE BREAD

Preparation Time: 5 minutes   **Cooking Time:** 3 hours   **Servings:** 3

INGREDIENTS

- Bread flour, 2 ½ cups
- Yeast, 2 ¼ tsp
- Warm water: 1 ¼ cup
- Rye flour, 1 cup
- Molasses, 1/3 cup
- Caraway seed, 1 tbsp
- Salt, ½ tsp
- Cocoa powder, 1/8 cup
- Vegetable oil, 1/8 cup

DIRECTIONS

1. In the order, put all the ingredients into the bread machine.
2. Start by selecting white bread.
3. Serve while it's fresh.

Nutritional Value: 105 Kcal, Protein: 10g, Carb: 4g, Fat: 6g
Note: This hearty rye bread has a deep flavor and is perfect for sandwiches or with hearty soups.

13. GOLDEN RAISIN BREAD

Preparation Time: 10 minutes   **Cooking Time:** 3 hours   **Servings:** 5

INGREDIENTS

- Oatmeal, 1 Cup
- Warm Milk, 1 1/3 Cups
- Bread Flour, 3 Cups
- Brown Sugar, ½ cup
- Bread Machine Yeast, 2 Tsp
- Sliced Butter, 4 Tbsp
- Molasses, 2 Tsp
- Golden Raisins, 1 Cup
- Salt, 2 Tsp

DIRECTIONS

1. In the sequence recommended by the manufacturer, put all ingredients into the bread maker, excluding the raisins.
2. Choose a 2 lb. loaf with a basic, light crust.
3. Start by pressing the button.
4. Put in raisins as the machine has finished its first round of mixing.
5. Serve while it's fresh.

Nutritional Value: 150 Kcal, Protein: 20g, Carb: 17g, Fat: 12g
Note: The sweetness of golden raisins adds a burst of flavor to this delicious bread.

14. GOLDEN CORN BREAD

Preparation Time: 10 minutes **Cooking Time:** 3 hours **Servings:** 4

INGREDIENTS

- Cornmeal, 1 cup
- Lightly beaten eggs, 2
- Softened butter, 1/4 cup
- Milk, 1 cup
- Bread flour, 1¼ cup
- Baking powder, 4 tsp
- Sugar, 1/4 cup
- Vanilla, 1 tsp
- Salt, 1 tsp

DIRECTIONS

1. As per the order, the manufacturer recommends. Put each of the ingredients into the bread maker.
2. If available, use the fast option or the light crust & cake option.
3. Start by pressing the button.
4. Serve while it's fresh.

Nutritional Value: 110 Kcal, Protein: 18g, Carb: 10g, Fat: 14g
Note: Made with cornmeal, this bread has a slightly sweet and moist texture.

15. ENGLISH MUFFIN BREAD

Preparation Time: 15 minutes **Cooking Time:** 3 hours 25 minutes **Servings:** 3

INGREDIENTS

- Lukewarm milk, 1 cup
- Vinegar, 1 tsp
- Butter, 2 tbsp
- Water, 1/3 cup
- Salt, 1½ tsp
- Instant yeast, 2¼ tsp
- All-purpose flour, 3½ cups
- Sugar, 1½ tsp
- Baking powder, ½ tsp

DIRECTIONS

1. Put all ingredients in the bread maker's pan. In humid surroundings, use less water, while in a dry or chilly setting, use more.
2. Pick a simple, light crust. Start by pressing the button. If the dough is too sticky, put in additional flour, and if it is too dry, put in water.
3. Serve while it's fresh.

Nutritional Value: 140 Kcal, Protein: 8g, Carb: 5g, Fat: 7g
Note: Enjoy the taste and texture of English muffins in the form of a loaf of bread.

16. TRADITIONAL ITALIAN BREAD

Preparation Time: 10 minutes **Cooking Time:** 3 hours **Servings:** 2

INGREDIENTS

- Sugar, 1 tbsp
- Cold Water, 3/4 cup
- Salt, 1 tsp
- Bread flour, 2 cups
- Dry yeast, 1 tsp
- Olive oil, 1 tbsp

DIRECTIONS

1. In the sequence recommended by the manufacturer, put each ingredient in the bread maker's pan.
2. Choose the basic cycle or the Italian cycle. Thin crust. Start by pressing the button.
3. Serve while it's fresh.

Nutritional Value: 120 Kcal, Protein: 2g, Carb: 3g, Fat: 4g
Note: This classic Italian bread is perfect for dipping in olive oil or making sandwiches.

17. COCOA BREAD

Preparation Time: 10 minutes **Cooking Time:** 3 hours **Servings:** 4

INGREDIENTS

- Egg, 1
- Yolk, 1
- Milk, 1 cup
- Canola oil, 3 tbsp
- Salt, 1 tsp
- Wheat gluten, 1 tbsp
- Vanilla extract, 1 tsp
- Brown sugar, ½ cup
- Yeast (bread machine), 2 ½ cup
- Bread flour, 3 cups
- Cocoa powder, 1/3 cup

DIRECTIONS

1. In the sequence recommended by the manufacturer, put each ingredient in the bread machine.
2. Choose the white bread, Med crust. Start by pressing the button.
3. Serve while it's fresh.

Nutritional Value: 125 Kcal, Protein: 24g, Carb: 17g, Fat: 16g
Note: Indulge in the rich chocolate flavor of this cocoa-infused bread.

18. GRANDMA'S CHRISTMAS BREAD

Preparation Time: 10 minutes **Cooking Time:** 3hrs **Servings:** 1

INGREDIENTS

- Lemon juice, 1/2 tsp
- Warm milk, 1¼ cups
- Melted butter, 2 tbsp
- Salt, 1½ tsp
- Sugar, 2 tbsp
- dry yeast, 2 tsp
- Golden raisins, 3/4 cup
- Bread flour, 3 cups
- Raisins, 3/4 cup
- lemon zest (Grated), 1½ tsp
- Dried currants, 1/2 cup
- **Glaze:**
- Confectioners' sugar, 1/2 cup
- Softened butter, 1 tsp
- Milk, 1½ tsp
- Vanilla extract, 1/4 tsp

DIRECTIONS

1. According to the maker's instructions, place the initial 7 ingredients in the machine's pan. Select a basic setting to bake the bread. If accessible, opt for the loaf size & colour of the crust. In accordance with the bread machine, cook.
2. Just before you finish kneading, put the currants, lemon zest & raisins. Mix the glaze ingredients in a small basin, then pour it on the chilled bread.

Nutritional Value: 130 Kcal, Protein: 4g, Carb: 3g, Fat: 5g
Note: Packed with raisins, currants, and lemon zest, this bread is perfect for the holiday season.

19. WHITE BREAD

Preparation Time: 10 minutes **Cooking Time:** 2hrs **Servings:** 10

INGREDIENTS

- Dry yeast, 1½ tsp
- Bread flour, 2 cups
- Salt, 1 tsp
- White sugar, 1 tbsp
- Dry milk powder, 1 tbsp
- Butter softened, 1 tbsp
- Water, ¾ cup

DIRECTIONS

1. As per the recommended order, Put the ingredients in the pan of the bread machine. Select the medium cycle, then press the Start button. After it has completed baking, take the bread out of the skillet, and let it cool.

Nutritional Value: 125 Kcal, Protein: 12g, Carb: 8g, Fat: 5g
Note: This simple and versatile white bread is a staple in many households.

20. WHITE BREAD II

Preparation Time: 15 minutes **Cooking Time:** 2hrs 40mins **Servings:** 12

INGREDIENTS

- Water, 1 cup
- Milk powder, 2 tbsp
- Bread flour, 3 cups
- White sugar, 2 tbsp
- Vegetable oil, 2 tbsp
- Salt, 1 tsp
- dry yeast, 1¼ tsp

DIRECTIONS

1. As per recommended order, put the ingredients in the pan of the bread machine, then select the basic Loop with White Bread and press the Start button.

Nutritional Value: 160 Kcal, Protein: 16g, Carb: 12g, Fat: 18g
Note: A straightforward recipe for delicious homemade white bread.

21. RON'S BREAD MACHINE WHITE

Preparation Time: 15 minutes **Cooking Time:** 3hrs **Servings:** 15

INGREDIENTS

- Vegetable oil, 2 tbsp
- Water, 1 cup
- Bread flour, 1 cup
- Salt, 1½ tsp
- Beaten large egg, 1
- Flour (All-purpose), 2 cups
- White sugar, 1 tbsp
- Dry milk powder, 2 tbsp
- Dry yeast, 1¼ tsp

DIRECTIONS

1. Put all of the ingredients in a sequence recommended by the maker, then choose the loaf's easy setting and the normal crust.

Nutritional Value: 85 Kcal, Protein: 3g, Carb: 5g, Fat: 8g
Note: Try this foolproof recipe for a tasty loaf of white bread.

22. ARGENTINIAN ROLLS

Preparation Time: 15 minutes   **Cooking Time:** 1 hour 25 mins   **Servings:** 4

INGREDIENTS

- Water (Warm), 280 ml
- Flour (Strong), 500 g
- Softened Pork lard, 65 g
- Salt, 10 g
- Dried yeast, 1½ tbsp
- Butter for coating

DIRECTIONS

1. To begin, place each ingredient in the bread machine, excluding the butter, and set it to 'dough.'
2. When done, place the dough on the surface that is floured and flatten it to remove any air bubbles.
3. Use the dough roller to roll the dough out to a thickness of 2.5 centimetres.

Nutritional Value: 105 Kcal, Protein: 6g, Carb: 3g, Fat: 2g
Note: These soft and fluffy rolls are perfect for sandwiches or as dinner rolls.

23. HOMEMADE SLIDER BUNS

Preparation Time: 20 minutes   **Cooking Time:** 2hrs   **Servings:** 18

INGREDIENTS

- Dry yeast, 2¼ tsp
- Milk, 2/3 cup
- Egg, 1
- Warm water, ½ cup
- Softened & chilled butter, 3 tbsp
- Sugar, 2½ tbsp
- Salt, 1¼ tsp
- Flour (all-purpose), 3 cups
- Oil to grease the bowl
- **Optional Toppings:**
- Egg, 1
- Water, 1 tbsp
- Poppy/Sesame seeds, ¼ cup
- Softened butter

DIRECTIONS

1. In a large mixing bowl, add yeast & warm water. Allow the combination to foam for around ten minutes.
2. In a tiny mixing bowl, stir in the egg, milk, & softened butter.
3. Combine the milk mixture with the yeast mixture, salt, flour & sugar.
4. Knead the dough with h& for eight to ten minutes, adding extra flour to prevent the dough from adhering to the bowl's sides. Now, the dough needs to be elastic and smooth.
5. Grease the big bowl using the oil or butter. Then roll the dough into a ball and set it in a greased bowl. After that, flip it over a couple of times to completely coat the dough.
6. With plastic wrap, Cover the bowl & let it aside for around one hour or until the dough has doubled.
7. Line a big cookie sheet using parchment paper or gently oil a baking pan.
8. Punch the dough down and press it into a rectangular shape.
9. Divide the dough into Eighteen pieces, each about 1 & half ounces.
10. Form the dough into tight balls, flatten slightly, & arrange them on the greased cookie sheet about two to three inches apart.
11. To Cover the buns, put the thin kitchen towel, and set them aside in a draft-free area to rise for about 30 minutes.
12. Preheat the oven's temperature to 375 degrees Fahrenheit. Coat every roll with an egg wash and drizzle with sesame/poppy seeds before putting it in the oven.
13. Bake for around 17 minutes, until it's golden brown. Coat it with softened butter if you have not used egg wash and seeds. Allow the buns to cool. Divide the buns and fill them with the contents.

Nutritional Value: 110 Kcal, Protein: 12g, Carb: 7g, Fat: 9g
Note: Make your own slider buns for mini burgers or sandwiches.

24. JEWISH BREAD MACHINE CHALLAH

Preparation Time: 15 minutes **Cooking Time:** 3 hrs **Servings:** 16

INGREDIENTS

- Salt, 1 ½ tsp
- beaten egg, 2
- beaten egg yolk, 1
- lukewarm water, 1 cup
- Honey, 1/2 cup
- Vegetable Oil, 2 ½ tbsp
- Bread Flour, 4 2/3 cups
- Yeast, 1 ¼ tsp

DIRECTIONS

1. In the bread pan, put the egg yolk, salt, oil, egg, honey, and water. Next, sprinkle flour over the liquid using a spoon. After this, put yeast.
2. Press Start after selecting the Basic/Sweet cycle and the Light Crust option.
3. Pause it at the beginning of the last rise, after which Take the dough out of the bread pan, place it on a floured board, and gently press it down.
4. Make thirds of the dough. After that, roll every third into a ten inches long rope. Afterward, lay those three ropes parallel to one another, close together but not contacting, on the floured surface. After that, tightly braid the ropes. Create an oblong loaf by tucking the ends under.
5. Then sprinkle sesame/poppy seeds on top of the braid after brushing it using a beaten egg. Put the seeds into the dough if you like.
6. The bread pan's kneading paddle(s) should be taken out. The cycle will then be continued by placing the braid in a skillet and pressing the Start button.
7. Once the bread concludes its baking, it should be transferred to the rack for thorough cooling before slicing.

Nutritional Value: 184 Kcal, Protein: 26g, Carb: 12g, Fat: 16g
Note: This traditional Jewish bread is slightly sweet and perfect for Sabbath and holidays.

25. GREEK LOAF

Preparation Time: 15 minutes **Cooking Time:** 3hrs **Servings:** 7

INGREDIENTS

- Milk, 1 cup
- Olive oil, 1 tbsp
- Salt, ½ tsp
- Feta cheese (Crumbled), 3/4 cup
- Bread flour, 3 cups
- Sugar, 1 tbsp
- Dry yeast, 2 ¼ tsp
- Ripe olives (Sliced), ¼ cup

DIRECTIONS

1. Add the initial seven ingredients to the pan of the bread maker. Select the standard bread setting. If desired, choose the loaf size and colour of the crust. Bake in accordance with the bread machine's instructions (after five minutes of mixing, make sure to check the dough and, if required, put 1 to 2 tbsp of flour/water).
2. Put the olives just before beginning the final kneading.

Nutritional Value: 145 Kcal, Protein: 15g, Carb: 13g, Fat: 17g
Note: With feta cheese and olives, this bread has a Greek-inspired flavor.

26. HALF HOUR BREAD

Preparation Time: 5 minutes   **Cooking Time:** 30 minutes   **Servings:** 4

INGREDIENTS

- Strong flour, 400 g
- Yeast, 14 g
- Milk, 200 g
- Lard, 1 tsp
- Melted butter, 15 g
- Sugar, 1 tsp
- Salt, 8 g

DIRECTIONS

1. First, stir this yeast into a cup of heated milk, sugar, as well as water.
2. Place that flour in the breadmaker's bowl and the salt in the flour pocket.
3. Add the yeast combination, butter, and lard.

Nutritional Value: 150 Kcal, Protein: 10g, Carb: 8g, Fat: 4g
Note: If you're in a hurry, this quick bread recipe can be ready in just 30 minutes.

4.2: Cheesy Breads

1. CHEESY CHIPOTLE BREAD

Preparation Time: 10 minutes   **Cooking Time:** 3 hours   **Servings:** 3

INGREDIENTS

- Salt, 1½ tsp
- Chipotle Chili powder, 1 tsp
- Mexican Cheese (Shredded), 1 cup
- lukewarm water, 1¼ cups
- Sugar, 1/4 cup
- Yeast (Bread machine), 1 tsp
- Dry milk, 3 tbsp
- Bread flour, 4 cups

DIRECTIONS

1. In the sequence recommended by its maker, add each ingredient to the pan of the bread maker.
2. Choose the white bread cycle with a thin crust. Start by pressing the button.
3. Avoid using delay cycles.
4. Serve while it's fresh.

Nutritional Value: 135 Kcal, Protein: 12g, Carb: 9g, Fat: 10g
Note: A flavorful bread with a kick of chipotle chili powder and gooey melted Mexican cheese.

2. ROASTED GARLIC ASIAGO BREAD

Preparation Time: 10 minutes   **Cooking Time:** 3 hours   **Servings:** 4

INGREDIENTS

- White bread flour, 1 cup
- Gluten flour, 1/4 cup
- Whole wheat flour, 1 3/4 cup
- Asiago cheese (grated), 3/4 cup
- Chopped rosemary, 2 tsp
- Dry milk, 2 tbsp
- Minced & roasted garlic cloves, 3
- Chopped basil, 1 tbsp
- Chopped oregano: 2 tsp
- Active dry yeast, 4 tsp
- Water, 1 1/4 cups
- Honey, 1 tsp
- Salt, 1 tsp
- Olive oil, 2 tbsp

DIRECTIONS

1. Place each of ingredients in the bread maker in the sequence the manufacturer specifies.
2. Choose the whole wheat cycle & customize the crust.
3. Serve while it's fresh.

Nutritional Value: 105 Kcal, Protein: 6g, Carb: 5g, Fat: 8g
Note: A savory bread with the rich flavors of roasted garlic and grated Asiago cheese.

3. CHEDDAR CHEESE BASIL BREAD

Preparation Time: 10 minutes   **Cooking Time:** 3 hours   **Servings:** 4

INGREDIENTS

- Melted butter (unsalted), 4 tbsp
- Shredded cheese, 1 cup
- Lukewarm milk, 2 tbsp
- Brown sugar, 1 tbsp
- Bread flour, 3 cups
- Basil, 1 tsp
- Salt, 1 1/2 tsp
- Yeast (bread machine), 1 1/2 tsp

DIRECTIONS

1. In the sequence, the manufacturer specifies. Add all the ingredients to the bread maker.
2. Choose the default setting and light crust. Start by pressing the button.
3. If desired, top a bit of cheese on a bread loaf before baking.
4. Serve while it's fresh.

Nutritional Value: 120 Kcal, Protein: 8g, Carb: 3g, Fat: 5g
Note: A delicious bread with melted cheddar cheese and aromatic basil.

4. JALAPEÑO CORN BREAD

Preparation Time: 10 minutes **Cooking Time:** 2 hours 40 minutes **Servings:** 2

INGREDIENTS

- Drained & Thawed corn (frozen), 2/3 cup
- Water, 2 tbsp plus ¾ cup
- Minced jalapeño chili, 1 tbsp
- Melted butter, 2 tbsp
- Sugar, 2 tbsp
- Bread flour, 3 ¼ cups
- Yeast (bread machine), 2 ½ tsp
- Cornmeal, 1/3 cup
- Salt, 1 ½ tsp

DIRECTIONS

1. Place each of the ingredients in the bread maker in the sequence the manufacturer specifies.
2. Select White cycle and Light crust—press start. Do not use a delay cycle.
3. Choose the white bread cycle with a thin crust. Start by pressing the button. Avoid using delay cycles.
4. Enjoy while it's fresh.

Nutritional Value: 85 Kcal, Protein: 17g, Carb: 21g, Fat: 26g
Note: A spicy and moist cornbread with jalapeño chili and a hint of sweetness.

5. OLIVE CHEESE BREAD

Preparation Time: 10 minutes **Cooking Time:** 4 hours **Servings:** 4

INGREDIENTS

- Olives (small stuffed), ½ cup
- Bread flour, 3 ¼ cups
- Chopped cheddar cheese, 1 cup
- Water, 1 cup
- Yeast, 1 ¼ tsp
- Salt, 1 tsp
- Sugar, 1 tsp

DIRECTIONS

1. Except for the olives, put all of the ingredients in the bread maker's pan. Choose basic. Start by pressing the button.
2. When 10 minutes are left in the kneading cycle, put in the olives.
3. Serve while it's fresh.

Nutritional Value: 110 Kcal, Protein: 5g, Carb: 8g, Fat: 6g
Note: A bread packed with small stuffed olives and cheddar cheese, perfect for snacking.

6. BLUE CHEESE ONION BREAD

Preparation Time: 10 minutes **Cooking Time:** 3 hours 40 minutes **Servings:** 3

INGREDIENTS

- Powdered milk, 3 tbsp
- Sugar, 2 tbsp
- Onion flakes (Dried), 2 tbsp
- Salt, ½ tsp
- Water, 1 1/3 cups
- Bread machine yeast, 1 ¼ tsp
- White flour, 4 cups
- Blue cheese (Shredded), 1/4 cup

DIRECTIONS

1. In the order the manufacturer recommends, put all the ingredients into the bread maker.
2. Press start after selecting the sweet bread cycle & dark crust, if desired.
3. Serve while it's fresh

Nutritional Value: 113 Kcal, Protein: 2g, Carb: 3g, Fat: 4g
Note: A unique bread combining dried onion flakes and tangy blue cheese for a bold flavor.

7. DOUBLE CHEESE BREAD

Preparation Time: 10 minutes **Cooking Time:** 3 hours **Servings:** 3

INGREDIENTS

- Bread flour, 3 cups
- Salt, 1 tsp
- Black pepper(coarse), 1 tsp
- Chopped cheddar cheese, 1 ½ cups
- Sugar, 2 tbsp
- Luke warm water, 1 ¼ cup
- Bread machine yeast, 1 ¼ tsp
- Melted butter, 1 tbsp
- Powder of Dry milk, 1/4 cup
- Thinly chopped Parmesan cheese, 1/3 cup

DIRECTIONS

1. Place all ingredients in the bread maker according to the manufacturer's recommended sequence.
2. Choose white bread with a medium crust. Start by pressing the button.
3. Shredded cheese should be sprinkled on top of the bread with 15-20 minutes of baking remaining.
4. Serve while it's fresh.

Nutritional Value: 130 Kcal, Protein: 20g, Carb: 18g, Fat: 14g
Note: A cheesy delight with both cheddar and Parmesan cheese, perfect for cheese lovers.

8. SALAMI & MOZZARELLA BREAD

Preparation Time: 10 minutes **Cooking Time:** 3 hours **Servings:** 3

INGREDIENTS

- Chopped mozzarella cheese, 1/3 cup
- Dried oregano, 1 ½ tsp
- Warm water, 1 cup + two tbsp
- Sugar, 2 tbsp
- Garlic salt, 1 ½ tsp
- Active dry yeast, 1 ½ tsp
- Diced salami, 2/3 cup
- Bread flour, 3 ¼ cups

DIRECTIONS

1. Except for the salami, place every ingredient in the bread maker in the sequence recommended by the manufacturer.
2. Choose the basic cycle. Avoid using the time delay.
3. Before the final kneading, put in the salami.
4. Enjoy while it's fresh.

Nutritional Value: 98 Kcal, Protein: 8g, Carb: 12g, Fat: 5g
Note: A bread loaded with diced salami and gooey mozzarella cheese for a savory treat.

Thank you from the bottom of my heart for choosing to read this book!

It is with immense gratitude that I address these words to you. It gives me enormous pleasure to know that you have decided to give your time and attention to these pages that I have written with commitment and dedication.

Creating this book has been an exciting journey, and my hope is that you have found it as enjoyable and inspiring to read as I have in writing it. Every word was carefully chosen with the goal of conveying a message, a story or a new perspective to you.

I am aware that you have a multitude of choices available to you when it comes to books, and the fact that you chose mine is a source of great pride and happiness. Your choice is invaluable to me, as it is the support and interest of readers like you that give meaning to my work as a writer.

If you have enjoyed the journey you have taken with these pages, I kindly ask you to **share your experience with others**. Reader reviews are a vital tool for raising awareness of a book and helping other readers make an informed choice.

If you feel inspired to do so, you might **take a few minutes to write a positive review** in which you could share your opinions. Even a few words can make a huge difference and help introduce the book to a wider audience.

9. COTTAGE CHEESE BREAD (SIMPLE)

Preparation Time: 10 minutes **Cooking Time:** 3 hours **Servings:** 2

INGREDIENTS

- Bread flour, 3 cups
- Water, 1/3 cup
- Butter, 2 Tbsp
- Cottage Cheese, 1 cup
- Egg, 1
- Sugar, 1 tbsp
- Yeast, 2 tsp
- Baking Soda, 1/4 tsp
- Salt, 1 tsp

DIRECTIONS

1. In the sequence that the manufacturer recommends, put all the ingredients into the bread maker.
2. Start by selecting a simple, light crust.
3. Enjoy it hot.

Nutritional Value: 90 Kcal, Protein: 4g, Carb: 7g, Fat: 5g
Note: A simple yet tasty bread made with cottage cheese, perfect for a quick snack or breakfast.

10. CHILE CHEESE BACON BREAD

Preparation Time: 10 minutes **Cooking Time:** 3 hours 10 minutes **Servings:** 4

INGREDIENTS

- Vegetable oil, 2 tbsp
- Bread flour, 4 cups
- Salt, 1¼ tsp
- Water, 1 1/3 cups
- Dry milk, 3 tbsp
- Mexican cheese, 2 cups
- Bacon bits, 3 tbsp
- Dry yeast, 2 tsp
- Sugar, 2 tbsp plus 1½ tsp.

DIRECTIONS

1. Except for the bacon & cheese, put all ingredients into the bread maker in the maker's recommended sequence.
2. Choose a basic setting and customize the crust.
3. At the fruit & nut signal, put in bacon.
4. Serve while it's fresh.

Nutritional Value: 150 Kcal, Protein: 24g, Carb: 21g, Fat: 12g
Note: A flavorful bread with Mexican cheese, bacon bits, and a touch of spice.

11. ITALIAN PARMESAN BREAD

Preparation Time: 10 minutes **Cooking Time:** 3 hours **Servings:** 4

INGREDIENTS

- All-purpose flour, 4 cups
- Parmesan cheese, ¼ cup
- Water, 1½ cups
- Salt, 1½ tsp
- Yeast, 2½ tsp
- Garlic powder, 1 tsp
- Seasoning of Italian pizza, 1 tsp

DIRECTIONS

1. Place all ingredients in the bread maker according to the manufacturer's recommended sequence.
2. Press start after selecting basic/delay cycle.
3. Serve while it's fresh

Nutritional Value: 120 Kcal, Protein: 21g, Carb: 10g, Fat: 8g
Note: A bread infused with the flavors of Parmesan cheese, garlic powder, and Italian seasoning.

12. RICH CHEDDAR BREAD

Preparation Time: 10 minutes **Cooking Time:** 3 hours **Servings:** 3

INGREDIENTS

- Parmesan cheese, 2½ tbsp
- Salt, ½ tsp
- Warm water, 1 cup
- Sugar, 3½ tsp
- Dry mustard, 1 tsp
- Melted butter, 2½ tbsp
- Chopped cheddar cheese, 1¼ cup
- Bread flour, 2½ cups
- Dry yeast, 2 tsp
- Paprika, 1½ tsp
- Chopped onions, 2½ tbsp

DIRECTIONS

1. Add each ingredient to the bread maker in the manufacturer's recommended sequence.
2. Choose the white option and customize the crust.
3. Select "Start" and check the dough's consistency to see if additional flour or water is needed.
4. Serve while it's fresh

Nutritional Value: 165 Kcal, Protein: 18g, Carb: 21g, Fat: 13g
Note: A hearty bread with chopped cheddar cheese, onions, and a touch of paprika.

13. FETA OREGANO BREAD

Preparation Time: 10 minutes **Cooking Time:** 3 hours **Servings:** 2

INGREDIENTS

- Olive oil, 1½ tbsp
- Bread flour, 3 cups
- Feta cheese (crumbled), ½ cup
- Water, 1 cup
- Dry yeast, 2 tsp
- Leaf oregano (dried), 1 tbsp
- Salt, 1 tsp
- Sugar, 3 tbsp

DIRECTIONS

1. Add each ingredient to the bread maker in the manufacturer's recommended sequence.
2. Choose basic. Start by pressing the button.
3. Serve while it's fresh.

Nutritional Value: 110 Kcal, Protein: 6g, Carb: 3g, Fat: 3g
Note: A Mediterranean-inspired bread with crumbled feta cheese and fragrant dried oregano.

14. GOAT CHEESE BREAD

Preparation Time: 10 minutes **Cooking Time:** 3 hours **Servings:** 4

INGREDIENTS

- Bread flour, 2 cups
- Water, 3/4 cup
- Dry yeast, 1½ tsp
- Granulated sugar, 1 tbsp
- Salt, ½ tsp
- Goat cheese (softened), 3 tbsp
- Dry milk (non-fat), 1 tbsp
- Cracked black pepper, 1½ tsp

DIRECTIONS

1. Each ingredient has to be at room temp.
2. Place all ingredients in the bread maker according to the manufacturer's recommended sequence.
3. Click "Start" and choose "Normal Cycle."
4. See the consistency of the dough; it shouldn't be too moist or too dry.
5. If necessary, put one tbsp of flour/Water.
6. Serve while it's fresh

Nutritional Value: 145 Kcal, Protein: 12g, Carb: 11g, Fat: 15g
Note: A bread featuring the tangy flavor of goat cheese and a hint of cracked black pepper.

15. MOZZARELLA-HERB BREAD

Preparation Time: 10 minutes **Cooking Time:** 3 hours **Servings:** 2

INGREDIENTS

- Onion Powder, 1 Tsp
- lukewarm milk, 1/3 Cup
- Sliced Butter, 6 Tbsp
- Yeast (Bread Machine), 1½ tsp
- Bread Flour, 4 Cups
- Sugar, 2 Tbsp
- Salt, 1½ Tsp
- Seasoning of Italian Herb, 2 Tbsp

DIRECTIONS

1. Place all ingredients in the bread maker according to the manufacturer's recommended sequence.
2. Click start after selecting basic, light crust.
3. Italian spice should be added to the top before the baking process starts.
4. Serve while it's fresh.

Nutritional Value: 130 Kcal, Protein: 10g, Carb: 7g, Fat: 8g
Note: A bread seasoned with Italian herb blend and topped with sliced butter for added richness.

4.3: Vegetable Bread

1. YEASTED CARROT BREAD

Preparation Time: 10 minutes **Cooking Time:** 4 hours 10 minutes **Servings:** 7

INGREDIENTS

- Whole wheat flour, 2/3 cup
- Rolled oats, 1 1/3 cup
- Bread flour, 2 cups
- Salt, 1 1/3 tsp
- Vegetable oil, 1 1/2 tbsp
- Water, 1 cup
- Brown sugar, 2 tbsp
- Dry milk powder, 1/4 cup
- Active dry yeast, 2 1/2 tsp
- Grated carrot, 2/3 cup

DIRECTIONS

1. Place all the ingredients into the bread machine according to the recommended order provided by the manufacturer.
2. Choose the basic setting with a light crust. Initiate the baking process.
3. Indulge in the delightful experience of savoring freshly baked bread.

Nutritional Value: 180 kcal, Protein: 5g, Carbs: 32g, Fat: 3g
Note: Yeasted Carrot Bread is a nutritious and flavourful bread made with grated carrots and whole wheat flour.

2. SAUERKRAUT RYE BREAD

Preparation Time: 10 minutes **Cooking Time:** 3 hours 50 minutes **Servings:** 7

INGREDIENTS

- Bread flour, 2 cups
- Sauerkraut (rinsed & drained), 1 cup
- Butter, 1 1/2 tbsp
- Warm water, 3/4 cup
- Brown sugar, 1 1/2 tbsp
- Active dry yeast, 1 1/2 tsp
- Molasses, 1 1/2 tbsp
- Salt, 1 1/2 tsp
- Caraway seed, 1 tsp
- Rye flour, 1 cup

DIRECTIONS

1. Place all the ingredients into the bread machine according to the recommended order provided by the manufacturer.
2. Choose the basic setting with a light crust. Initiate the baking process.
3. Indulge in the delightful experience of savoring freshly baked bread.

Nutritional Value: 150 kcal, Protein: 4g, Carbs: 28g, Fat: 2g
Note: Sauerkraut Rye Bread is a flavourful and tangy bread made with sauerkraut and rye flour.

3. SAVOURY ONION BREAD

Preparation Time: 10 minutes **Cooking Time:** 3 hours 40 minutes **Servings:** 7

INGREDIENTS

For Caramelized Onions:
- Sliced onions, 2
- Butter, 1 tbsp

For Bread:
- Water, 1 cup
- Olive oil, 1 tbsp
- Bread flour, 3 cups
- Sugar, 2 tbsp
- Salt, 1 tsp
- Bread machine yeast, 1 1/4 tsp

DIRECTIONS

1. In a pan, sauté onions over medium heat in butter until they are caramelized and golden brown. Turn off the heat.
2. Add all the bread ingredients to the bread machine in the recommended order by the manufacturer, except for the caramelized onions.
3. Select the Basic cycle and press start. Avoid using the delay feature.
4. Add half a cup of the caramelized onions at the nut signal.
5. Serve the freshly baked bread.

Nutritional Value: 160 kcal, Protein: 4g, Carbs: 31g, Fat: 3g
Note: Savoury Onion Bread is a delicious and aromatic bread with caramelized onions.

4. TOMATO HERB BREAD

Preparation Time: 10 minutes   **Cooking Time:** 4 hours 10 minutes   **Servings:** 7

INGREDIENTS

- Whole egg, 1
- Olive oil, 2 tbsp
- Dried minced onion, 2 tsp
- Warm milk, 1/2 cup + 2 tbsp (70°-80° F)
- Salt, 1/2 tsp
- Minced fresh parsley, 2 tbsp
- Sugar, 1 tbsp
- Active dry yeast, 2 1/4 tsp
- Garlic powder, 1/2 tsp
- Tomato paste, 1 can (6 ounces)
- Dried tarragon, 1/2 tsp
- Bread flour, 3 cups

DIRECTIONS

1. Combine all the ingredients in the bread machine according to the recommended order provided by the manufacturer.
2. Select the basic bread setting and adjust the crust preference as desired.
3. After a duration of five minutes, assess the dough's consistency and incorporate additional flour if it exhibits excessive moisture and stickiness.
4. If necessary, include one tablespoon of flour.
5. Enjoy the freshly baked bread.

Nutritional Value: 160 kcal, Protein: 5g, Carbs: 29g, Fat: 2g
Note: Tomato Herb Bread is a flavourful bread with a hint of tomato and aromatic herbs.

5. MASHED POTATO BREAD

Preparation Time: 10 minutes   **Cooking Time:** 3 hours 15 minutes   **Servings:** 7

INGREDIENTS

- Dry milk powder, 1 tbsp
- Sunflower oil, 2 tbsp
- White bread flour, 3 1/4 cups
- Salt, 1 tsp
- Potato cooking water at room temperature, 0.8 cup
- Mashed potatoes, 1 1/2 cups
- Active dry yeast, 1 1/2 tsp
- Sugar, 2 tbsp

DIRECTIONS

1. Combine all the listed ingredients in the bread machine following the recommended order provided by the manufacturer.
2. Choose the basic setting with a medium crust and initiate the baking process.
3. Apply a milk glaze to the bread using a brush at the beginning of the cooking time.
4. Serve the freshly baked bread.

Nutritional Value: 170 kcal, Protein: 5g, Carbs: 33g, Fat: 2g
Note: Mashed Potato Bread is a soft and moist bread made with mashed potatoes.

6. CONFETTI BREAD

Preparation Time: 10 minutes   **Cooking Time:** 3 hours 10 minutes   **Servings:** 7

INGREDIENTS

- Instant skim-milk powder, 2 tsp
- Roughly chopped old cheddar cheese, 3/4 cup
- Salt, 3/4 tsp
- Sugar, 1 tsp
- Water, 3/4 cup
- Shredded carrot, 1/2 cup
- White flour, 3 cups
- Bread machine yeast, 1 1/4 tsp
- Diced sweet mix bell pepper, 1/3 cup
- Dried Italian seasoning, 2 tsp

DIRECTIONS

1. Put all the ingredients, except for the cheese, into the bread machine following the recommended order provided by the manufacturer.
2. Choose the white bread cycle and start the machine.
3. Add the cheese when the ingredient signal prompts.
4. Enjoy the freshly baked bread.

Nutritional Value: 180 kcal, Protein: 7g, Carbs: 33g, Fat: 2g
Note: Confetti Bread is a delightful and colourful bread with added vegetables and cheddar cheese.

7. PRETTY BORSCHT BREAD

Preparation Time: 10 minutes   **Cooking Time:** 3 hours 10 minutes   **Servings:** 7

INGREDIENTS

- Onion soup mix (dry), 1 package
- Tomato juice, 2/3 cup
- Ground ginger, 1/4 tsp
- Active dry yeast, 2 1/4 tsp
- All-purpose flour, 3 cups
- Grated carrot, 1/3 cup
- Wheat germ, 1 tbsp
- Vegetable oil, 2 tbsp
- Beet, cooked & chopped, 3/4 cup
- Sour cream, 1/2 cup
- Granulated sugar, 1/4 tsp

DIRECTIONS

1. Combine all ingredients in the bread machine following the manufacturer's recommended order.
2. Choose the dough cycle.
3. Remove the dough from the machine and allow it to rise for one and a half hours.
4. Deflate the dough and let it rise again for 60 minutes.
5. Preheat the oven to 350°F.
6. Bake the bread for 20-25 minutes.
7. Serve the freshly baked bread.

Nutritional Value: 160 kcal, Protein: 4g, Carbs: 30g, Fat: 3g
Note: Pretty Borscht Bread is a unique and vibrant bread inspired by the flavours of borscht soup. It incorporates beets and sour cream to create a distinct and delightful taste.

8. YEASTED PUMPKIN BREAD

Preparation Time: 10 minutes   **Cooking Time:** 3 hours 5 minutes   **Servings:** 7

INGREDIENTS

- Mashed pumpkin puree, 1 cup
- Salt, 1 1/4 tsp
- Sugar, 2 tbsp
- Bread flour, 4 cups
- Milk, 1/2 cup + 2 tbsp
- Active dry yeast, 2 1/4 tsp
- Vegetable oil, 2 tbsp

DIRECTIONS

1. Add all the ingredients to the bread machine pan following the recommended order provided by the manufacturer.
2. Choose the white bread setting and select the light crust option. Begin the baking process.
3. Indulge in the delight of freshly baked bread.

Nutritional Value: 160 kcal, Protein: 4g, Carbs: 32g, Fat: 2g
Note: Yeasted Pumpkin Bread is a flavourful and moist bread made with pumpkin puree.

9. OATMEAL ZUCCHINI BREAD

Preparation Time: 10 minutes   **Cooking Time:** 2 hours 10 minutes   **Servings:** 7

INGREDIENTS

- Eggs, 2
- Packed brown sugar, 1/3 cup
- Shredded zucchini, 3/4 cup
- Granulated sugar, 3 tbsp
- All-purpose flour, 1 1/2 cups
- Vegetable oil, 1/3 cup
- Ground cinnamon, 3/4 tsp
- Baking powder, 1/2 tsp
- Salt, 3/4 tsp
- Ground allspice, 1/4 tsp
- Raisins, 1/3 cup
- Baking soda, 1/2 tsp
- Oatmeal, 1/3 cup

DIRECTIONS

1. Combine all the ingredients in the bread machine according to the recommended order provided by the manufacturer.
2. Make sure that all the ingredients are at room temperature.
3. Choose the Cake/Quick bread setting and initiate the baking process.
4. After 5 minutes, use a rubber spatula to scrape off any residue from the pan's surface and allow the cycle to proceed.
5. Serve the freshly baked bread.

Nutritional Value: 160 kcal, Protein: 3g, Carbs: 25g, Fat: 6g
Note: Oatmeal Zucchini Bread is a moist and hearty bread with the goodness of zucchini and the added texture of oatmeal.

10. HOT RED PEPPER BREAD

Preparation Time: 10 minutes **Cooking Time:** 3 hours 10 minutes **Servings:** 7

INGREDIENTS

- Butter, 1 tbsp
- Unsweetened yogurt, 2 tbsp
- Garlic cloves, 2
- Bread flour, 3 cups
- Parmesan cheese, 3 tbsp
- Roasted red pepper, 1/4 cup, chopped
- Dried basil, 1 1/2 tsp
- Water, 3/4 cup
- Sugar, 2 tbsp
- Bread machine yeast, 2 tsp
- Salt, 1 1/2 tsp

DIRECTIONS

1. Combine all the ingredients in the bread machine following the recommended order provided by the manufacturer.
2. Choose the basic setting with a light crust. Initiate the bread-making process.
3. Enjoy the freshly baked bread.

Nutritional Value: 150 kcal, Protein: 5g, Carbs: 29g, Fat: 2g
Note: Hot Red Pepper Bread is a flavourful and slightly spicy bread made with roasted red peppers and Parmesan cheese.

11. FRENCH ONION BREAD

Preparation Time: 10 minutes **Cooking Time:** 3 hours 10 minutes **Servings:** 7

INGREDIENTS

- Unsalted butter, 4 tbsp (softened)
- Diced and fried onion, 1/2
- Onion powder, 1 tbsp
- Bread flour, 3 cups
- Bread machine yeast, 1 1/2 tsp
- Lukewarm milk, 1 cup
- White sugar, 1 tbsp
- Salt, 1 1/2 tsp

DIRECTIONS

1. Add all ingredients to the bread machine in the suggested order by the manufacturer.
2. Select the basic setting. Light crust. Press start.
3. Enjoy fresh bread.

Nutritional Value: 170 kcal, Protein: 5g, Carbs: 31g, Fat: 3g
Note: French Onion Bread is a savoury and aromatic bread with the flavours of caramelized onions.

12. GOLDEN BUTTERNUT SQUASH RAISIN BREAD

Preparation Time: 10 minutes **Cooking Time:** 3 hours 10 minutes **Servings:** 7

INGREDIENTS

- Bread flour, 3 cups
- Non-fat milk powder, 3 tbsp
- Active dry yeast, 4 tsp
- Wheat germ, 3 tbsp
- Gluten flour, 3 tbsp
- Salt, 1 1/2 tsp
- Butter, 3 tbsp
- Butternut puree, 1 cup
- Water, 2/3 cup
- Raisins, 1/2 cup
- Sugar, 4 tbsp
- Ground ginger, 1/2 tsp
- Ground cinnamon, 3/4 tsp

DIRECTIONS

1. Add all ingredients to the bread machine in the suggested order by the manufacturer.
2. Select the basic setting. Choose the crust to your liking. Press start.
3. Serve fresh bread.

Nutritional Value: 160 kcal, Protein: 6g, Carbs: 32g, Fat: 2g
Note: Golden Butternut Squash Raisin Bread is a moist and flavourful bread with the sweetness of butternut squash and the added texture of raisins.

13. SWEET POTATO BREAD

Preparation Time: 10 minutes **Cooking Time:** 3 hours 10 minutes **Servings:** 7

INGREDIENTS

- Cinnamon, 1/2 tsp
- Lukewarm water, 1/2 cup
- Bread flour, 4 cups
- Vanilla extract, 1 tsp
- Packed brown sugar, 1/3 cup
- Butter, 2 tbsp (softened)
- Salt, 1 1/2 tsp
- Mashed sweet potatoes, 1 cup
- Powdered milk, 2 tbsp
- Yeast, 2 tsp

DIRECTIONS

1. Add all ingredients to the bread machine in the suggested order by the manufacturer.
2. Select the white bread setting with a light crust. Press start.
3. Serve fresh bread.

Nutritional Value: 170 kcal, Protein: 5g, Carbs: 34g, Fat: 2g
Note: Sweet Potato Bread is a moist and flavourful bread with the natural sweetness of sweet potatoes.

14. POTATO THYME BREAD

Preparation Time: 10 minutes   **Cooking Time:** 3 hours 10 minutes   **Servings:** 7

INGREDIENTS

- Salt, 1 1/2 tsp
- Butter, 2 tbsp (softened)
- Sugar, 1 tbsp
- Lukewarm water, 1 1/4 cups
- Bread machine yeast, 2 tsp
- Instant potato flakes, 1/2 cup
- Bread flour, 3 cups
- Dried thyme leaves, 2 tbsp

DIRECTIONS

1. Add all ingredients to the bread machine in the suggested order by the manufacturer.
2. Select the white cycle and choose a dark crust if desired.
3. Press start.
4. Serve fresh bread.

Nutritional Value: 160 kcal, Protein: 4g, Carbs: 31g, Fat: 2g
Note: Potato Thyme Bread is a flavourful and aromatic bread with the subtle taste of thyme and the richness of potatoes.

15. CORN BREAD

Preparation Time: 10 minutes   **Cooking Time:** 3 hours 10 minutes   **Servings:** 7

INGREDIENTS

- Milk, 1 cup
- Sugar, 1/4 cup
- Eggs (lightly whisked), 2
- Bread flour, 1 1/4 cups
- Baking powder, 4 tsp
- Cornmeal, 1 cup
- Melted butter, 1/4 cup
- Salt, 1 tsp
- Vanilla, 1 tsp

DIRECTIONS

1. Add all ingredients to the bread machine in the suggested order by the manufacturer.
2. Use the cake cycle/quick cycle and choose a light crust. Press start.
3. Serve fresh bread.

Nutritional Value: 150 kcal, Protein: 4g, Carbs: 25g, Fat: 4g
Note: Light Corn Bread is a fluffy and tender bread with a subtle sweetness and the delicious flavor of cornmeal.

4.4: Ketogenic Bread

1. BASIC LOW-CARB BREAD

Preparation Time: 10 minutes   **Cooking Time:** 3 hours 40 minutes   **Servings:** 7

INGREDIENTS

- Bread Machine Yeast, 1 1/2 tsp
- Sugar, 1 1/2 tbsp
- Vegetable Oil, 1/4 cup
- Warm Water, 1 cup
- Low Carb Flour, 3 cups
- Wheat Gluten, 3 tsp

DIRECTIONS

1. Apply cooking spray to the bread machine pan.
2. Activate yeast in warm water with sugar. After 8-10 minutes, pour it into the pan.
3. Add the remaining ingredients to the recommended order provided by the manufacturer.
4. Choose the low-carb cycle or basic setting. Initiate the baking process.
5. Delight in the delightful aroma and taste of freshly baked bread.

Nutritional Value: 120 kcal, Protein: 6g, Carbs: 6g, Fat: 8g
Note: Basic Low-Carb Bread is a great option for those following a low-carb lifestyle. It is made with low-carb flour and contains minimal carbohydrates.

2. ALMOND FLOUR YEAST BREAD

Preparation Time: 10 minutes   **Cooking Time:** 3 hours 40 minutes   **Servings:** 7

INGREDIENTS

- Almond Flour, 2 1/4 cups
- Water, 1 1/4 cups
- Psyllium Husk Powder, 1/3 cup
- Ground Flax Seed, 3/4 cup
- Wheat Gluten, 1/2 cup
- Coconut Palm Sugar, 2 tsp
- Seed Mix, 1/3 cup
- Eggs (lightly whisked), 6
- Yeast, 2 tbsp
- Extra Virgin Olive Oil, 2 tbsp
- Sea Salt, 1 tsp

DIRECTIONS

1. Combine all the ingredients in the bread machine according to the recommended sequence provided by the manufacturer.
2. Choose either a gluten-free or basic cycle and select a medium crust. Initiate the baking process by pressing the start button.
3. Once the kneading cycle is complete, use a rubber spatula to scrape the sides of the pan.
4. Indulge in the delightful taste of freshly baked bread.

Nutritional Value: 190 kcal, Protein: 9g, Carbs: 7g, Fat: 15g
Note: Almond Flour Yeast Bread is a delicious gluten-free option made with the goodness of almond flour. It has a nutty flavor and a moist texture, making it perfect for sandwiches or toast.

3. ALMOND MILK BREAD

Preparation Time: 10 minutes **Cooking Time:** 3 hours 20 minutes **Servings:** 7

INGREDIENTS

- Salt, 1 1/2 tsp
- Unsalted Butter (sliced into pieces), 1 tbsp
- Fast-Rising Yeast, 2 tsp
- Almond Flour, 3 cups
- Almond Milk, 1 1/8 cups
- Sugar, 1 tbsp
- Xanthan Gum, 1 tsp

DIRECTIONS

1. Place all the ingredients into the bread machine in the recommended sequence provided by the manufacturer.
2. Choose the basic cycle and select a medium crust option. Press the start button.
3. Delight in the delectable aroma and taste of freshly baked bread.

Nutritional Value: 160 kcal, Protein: 7g, Carbs: 7g, Fat: 13g
Note: Almond Milk Bread is a flavourful and moist bread made with almond flour and almond milk. It is a great option for those following a gluten-free or dairy-free diet.

4. FLAXSEED BREAD

Preparation Time: 10 minutes **Cooking Time:** 3 hours 40 minutes **Servings:** 7

INGREDIENTS

- Ground Flax Seed, 1/2 cup
- Bread Machine Yeast, 2 tsp
- Honey, 3 tbsp
- Warm Water, 1 1/3 cup
- Salt, 1 1/2 tsp
- Vegetable Oil, 2 tbsp
- Gluten-Free Flour, 1 1/2 cups
- Almond Flour, 1 1/3 cup

DIRECTIONS

1. Combine all the ingredients in the bread machine according to the recommended order provided by the manufacturer.
2. Choose the basic cycle and adjust the crust settings to your preference. Initiate the baking process.
3. Enjoy the freshly baked bread.

Nutritional Value: 140 kcal, Protein: 5g, Carbs: 13g, Fat: 8g
Note: Flaxseed Bread is a nutritious and gluten-free option packed with the goodness of flax seeds. It has a nutty flavor and a soft texture, making it perfect for sandwiches or as a side with soups or salads.

5. ALMOND FLOUR BREAD

Preparation Time: 10 minutes   **Cooking Time:** 3 hours 40 minutes   **Servings:** 7

INGREDIENTS

- Ground Flaxseed Meal, 1/4 cup
- Eggs (4 whole + 1 egg white)
- Baking Soda, 1 tsp
- Cinnamon, 1 tsp
- Apple Cider Vinegar, 1 tbsp
- Honey, 2 tbsp
- Coconut Oil, 2 tbsp
- Kosher Salt, 1/2 tsp
- Blanched Almond Flour, 2 1/2 cups

DIRECTIONS

1. Combine all the ingredients in the bread machine according to the recommended order provided by the manufacturer.
2. Choose the basic cycle and adjust the crust settings to your preference. Initiate the baking process.
3. Enjoy the freshly baked bread.

Nutritional Value: 160 kcal, Protein: 7g, Carbs: 7g, Fat: 13g
Note: Almond Flour Bread is a nutritious and gluten-free option made with almond flour.

6. SANDWICH BREAD

Preparation Time: 10 minutes   **Cooking Time:** 3 hours 30 minutes   **Servings:** 7

INGREDIENTS

- Sugar, 3 tbsp
- Half and Half, 1/3 cup
- Softened Butter, 3 tbsp
- Salt, 1 1/2 tsp
- Milk, 1 cup
- Instant Yeast, 1 1/2 tsp
- Almond Flour, 3 3/4 cups
- Xanthan Gum, 1 tsp

DIRECTIONS

1. Combine all the ingredients in the bread machine according to the recommended order provided by the manufacturer.
2. Choose the basic cycle and adjust the crust settings to your preference. Initiate the baking process.
3. Enjoy the freshly baked bread.

Nutritional Value: 180 kcal, Protein: 8g, Carbs: 11g, Fat: 12g
Note: Sandwich Bread is a versatile and fluffy bread that is perfect for making sandwiches.

7. MACADAMIA BREAD

Preparation Time: 10 minutes **Cooking Time:** 3 hours 40 minutes **Servings:** 7

INGREDIENTS

- Very Ripe Bananas, 3/4 cup
- Warm Water (110°F), 2/3 cup
- Softened Butter, 2 tbsp
- Macadamia Nuts (Ground), 1/2 cup
- Egg, 1
- White Sugar, 3 tbsp
- Bread Machine Yeast, 2 3/4 tsp
- Salt, 1 1/4 tsp
- Almond Flour, 3 1/4 cups
- Xanthan Gum, 1 1/4 tsp
- **For Glaze:**
- Sliced Almonds, 1/4 cup
- Egg Yolk, 1 (whisked with 1 tsp water)

DIRECTIONS

1. Place all components into the bread machine following the recommended sequence provided by the manufacturer.
2. Choose the white bread cycle and initiate the process by pressing the start button.
3. Once the rising cycle is complete, apply a yolk glaze and scatter the almonds on the surface.
4. Serve the freshly baked bread.

Nutritional Value: 210 kcal, Protein: 7g, Carbs: 15g, Fat: 15g
Note: Macadamia Bread is a delightful bread with a hint of sweetness and a rich nutty flavor from the macadamia nuts.

8. TOASTING BREAD

Preparation Time: 10 minutes **Cooking Time:** 2 hours 50 minutes **Servings:** 7

INGREDIENTS

- Water, 1/4-1/3 cup
- Vinegar, 1 tsp
- Lukewarm Milk, 1 cup
- Baking Powder, 1/2 tsp
- Salt, 1 1/2 tsp
- Instant Yeast, 2 1/4 tsp
- All-Purpose Flour, 3 1/2 cups
- Vegetable Oil, 2 tbsp
- Sugar, 1 1/2 tsp

DIRECTIONS

1. Combine all the ingredients in the bread machine following the recommended order provided by the manufacturer.
2. Adjust the amount of water as needed based on the climate conditions (reduce water in warm climates and increase in cold climates).
3. Choose the basic white bread cycle and start the machine.
4. Prior to the baking cycle, remove the dough from the machine and optionally roll it in cornmeal. Return the dough to the machine and allow it to bake.
5. Enjoy the freshly baked bread.

Nutritional Value: 150 kcal, Protein: 4g, Carbs: 26g, Fat: 3g
Note: Toasting Bread is a versatile bread that is perfect for toasting. It has a light and fluffy texture, making it ideal for spreading with butter, jams, or other toppings.

9. MEDITERRANEAN BREAD

Preparation Time: 10 minutes **Cooking Time:** 3 hours 40 minutes **Servings:** 7

INGREDIENTS

- Crumbled Feta Cheese, 1/3 cup
- Water, 1 cup
- Almond Flour, 3 1/4 cups
- Salt, 1 1/4 tsp
- Honey, 1 tbsp
- Extra Virgin Olive Oil, 1 tbsp
- Dried Oregano, 2 tsp
- Bread Machine Yeast, 3/4 tsp
- Minced Garlic, 3 cloves
- Sliced Kalamata Olives, 1/2 cup
- Xanthan Gum, 1 1/4 tsp

DIRECTIONS

1. Place all the ingredients in the bread machine following the recommended order provided by the manufacturer.
2. Choose the basic cycle and start the process.
3. Indulge in this delightful bread that complements Mediterranean-inspired meals perfectly.

Nutritional Value: 200 kcal, Protein: 9g, Carbs: 13g, Fat: 14g
Note: Mediterranean Bread is a flavourful and hearty bread with the addition of feta cheese, olives, and aromatic herbs.

10. ITALIAN ALPERITO BREAD

Preparation Time: 10 minutes **Cooking Time:** 3 hours 40 minutes **Servings:** 7

INGREDIENTS

- Salt, 1 1/2 tsp
- Gluten-Free Whole Wheat Flour, 4 1/4 cups
- Sugar, 2 tbsp
- Water, 1 1/2 cups
- Bread Machine Yeast, 2 tsp
- Olive Oil, 2 tbsp
- Xanthan Gum, 2 tsp

DIRECTIONS

1. Add all the listed ingredients into the bread machine following the recommended order provided by the manufacturer.
2. Choose the whole wheat cycle and initiate the process by pressing the start button.
3. Serve the freshly baked bread promptly.

Nutritional Value: 180 kcal, Protein: 5g, Carbs: 36g, Fat: 2g
Note: Italian Bread is a classic bread with a crispy crust and soft interior. It is perfect for serving Italian dishes or as a base for sandwiches.

11. KETO BAGUETTE

Preparation Time: 10 minutes   **Cooking Time:** 2 hours 40 minutes   **Servings:** 7

INGREDIENTS

- Warm Water, 1 1/4 cups
- Salt, 1 tsp
- Gluten-Free Flour, 3 1/2 cups
- Xanthan Gum, 1 1/2 tsp
- Active Dry Yeast, 1 package

DIRECTIONS

1. Combine all the ingredients in the bread machine following the recommended order provided by the manufacturer.
2. Choose the dough cycle and start the machine.
3. Transfer the dough to a clean surface dusted with flour.
4. Divide the dough into two equal portions and shape each portion into a 12" long baguette.
5. Place the baguettes on a greased baking pan and cover them with a warm towel.
6. Allow the baguettes to rise for approximately one hour while preheating the oven to 450°F.
7. Bake the baguettes for 15-20 minutes or until they turn a golden-brown colour.
8. Serve the freshly baked baguettes.

Nutritional Value: 180 kcal, Protein: 5g, Carbs: 36g, Fat: 2g
Note: Keto Baguette is a low-carb alternative to traditional baguettes. It is perfect for sandwiches or as a side with soups and salads.

12. KETO BRIOCHE BREAD

Preparation Time: 10 minutes   **Cooking Time:** 2 hours 40 minutes   **Servings:** 7

INGREDIENTS

- Keto-Flour, 1 3/4 cups
- Whole Eggs + 1 Yolk, 2
- Active Dry Yeast, 1 3/4 tsp
- Sugar, 3 tbsp
- Salt, 3/4 tsp
- Unsalted Butter, 8 tbsp
- Almond Flour, 2 tbsp
- Water, 1/4 cup
- Water, 2 tbsp

DIRECTIONS

1. Add all ingredients, except butter, to the bread machine in the suggested order by the manufacturer.
2. Select the basic bread cycle. Press start.
3. Cut butter into small pieces.
4. After the first kneading cycle, add one tablespoon of butter at a time.
5. Enjoy fresh bread.

Nutritional Value: 200 kcal, Protein: 5g, Carbs: 36g, Fat: 2g
Note: Keto Brioche Bread is a delicious low-carb bread with a rich buttery flavor.

13. OREGANO ONION FOCACCIA

Preparation Time: 10 minutes   **Cooking Time:** 3 hours 40 minutes   **Servings:** 7

INGREDIENTS

- **Dough:**
- Water, 3/4 cup
- Sugar, 1 tbsp
- Olive Oil, 2 tbsp
- Yeast, 1 1/2 tsp
- Salt, 1 tsp
- Shredded Parmesan Cheese, 2 tbsp
- Shredded Mozzarella Cheese, 3/4 cup
- Almond Flour, 2 cups
- Xanthan Gum, 3/4 tsp
- **Toppings:**
- Minced Garlic Cloves, 2
- Butter, 3 tbsp
- Sliced Onions, 2 medium

DIRECTIONS

1. Combine all dough ingredients in the bread machine according to the manufacturer's recommended order.
2. Choose the dough cycle and start the machine.
3. Meanwhile, melt butter over medium heat and sauté garlic and onion until they turn golden and flavourful.
4. Transfer the dough onto a baking sheet greased with oil.
5. Shape the dough into a 12" circle and allow it to rise for 30 minutes until it doubles in size.
6. Preheat the oven to 400°F.
7. Using a wooden spoon, create indentations in the dough.
8. Spread the caramelized onion and garlic mixture evenly over the dough.
9. Bake for 15-20 minutes until the bread turns a delightful golden brown.
10. Serve the freshly baked bread.

Nutritional Value: 200 kcal, Protein: 7g, Carbs: 12g, Fat: 2g
Note: Oregano Onion Focaccia is a savoury and aromatic bread with a delightful combination of flavours.

14. KETO FOCACCIA

Preparation Time: 10 minutes **Cooking Time:** 3 hours 10 minutes **Servings:** 7

INGREDIENTS

- Whole Wheat Flour, 3 cups
- Lukewarm Water, 1 cup
- Chopped Garlic, 2 tsp
- Active Dry Yeast, 1 1/2 tsp
- Olive Oil, 2 tbsp
- Chopped Fresh Rosemary, 1 tbsp
- Salt, 1/2 tsp
- Chopped Fresh Rosemary, 1 1/2 tsp
- Xanthan Gum, 1 tsp

DIRECTIONS

1. Combine all ingredients in the bread machine according to the manufacturer's recommended sequence.
2. Choose the dough cycle and initiate the process.
3. Transfer the dough to a 12" pizza pan once it has finished kneading.
4. Using your clean fingers, create dimples in the dough.
5. Brush the dough with olive oil and sprinkle it with fresh rosemary.
6. Cover the dough with plastic wrap and allow it to rise for 45 minutes.
7. Preheat your oven to 400°F.
8. Bake the dough for 20-25 minutes or until it turns a golden-brown colour.
9. Serve the freshly baked bread.

Nutritional Value: 220 kcal, Protein: 5g, Carbs: 36g, Fat: 2g
Note: Keto Focaccia is a flavourful and versatile bread that is perfect for serving as an appetizer, snack, or accompaniment to meals.

15. ZUCCHINI CIABATTA

Preparation Time: 10 minutes **Cooking Time:** 3 hours 40 minutes **Servings:** 7

INGREDIENTS

- Salt, 1 1/2 tsp
- Water, 1 1/2 cups
- Yeast, 1 1/2 tsp
- Olive Oil, 1 tbsp
- Bread flour, 3 1/4 cups
- Sugar, 1 tsp
- Grated Zucchini, 1/2 cup

DIRECTIONS

1. Ensure proper drying of the grated zucchini.
2. Add all the ingredients to the bread machine in the recommended order provided by the manufacturer.
3. Choose the dough cycle and initiate the process.
4. Once the dough cycle is finished, remove the dough without incorporating additional flour.
5. Transfer the dough to a floured bowl, cover it with plastic wrap, and let it rest for 15 minutes.
6. Place the dough on a floured surface and divide it into two equal halves.
7. Shape each half into an oval measuring 13" by 14" and allow it to rise for 45 minutes, covering it with a towel.
8. Preheat the oven to 425°F.
9. Create indentations on the dough and position it on the middle rack of the oven.
10. Bake for approximately 30 minutes, spraying water every 5-10 minutes throughout the baking process.
11. Serve the freshly baked bread.

Nutritional Value: 220 kcal, Protein: 3g, Carbs: 36g, Fat: 2g
Note: Zucchini Ciabatta is a flavourful and moist bread with a subtle hint of zucchini. It is perfect for sandwiches or served alongside soups and stews.

Thank you from the bottom of my heart for choosing to read this book!

It is with immense gratitude that I address these words to you. It gives me enormous pleasure to know that you have decided to give your time and attention to these pages that I have written with commitment and dedication.

Creating this book has been an exciting journey, and my hope is that you have found it as enjoyable and inspiring to read as I have in writing it. Every word was carefully chosen with the goal of conveying a message, a story or a new perspective to you.

I am aware that you have a multitude of choices available to you when it comes to books, and the fact that you chose mine is a source of great pride and happiness. Your choice is invaluable to me, as it is the support and interest of readers like you that give meaning to my work as a writer.

If you have enjoyed the journey you have taken with these pages, I kindly ask you to **share your experience with others**. Reader reviews are a vital tool for raising awareness of a book and helping other readers make an informed choice.

If you feel inspired to do so, you might **take a few minutes to write a positive review** in which you could share your opinions. Even a few words can make a huge difference and help introduce the book to a wider audience.

4.5: Sourdough Bread

1. SIMPLE SOURDOUGH STARTER (NO-YEAST WHOLE WHEAT SOURDOUGH STARTER)

Preparation Time: 10 minutes **Cooking Time:** 8 Days **Servings:** 8

INGREDIENTS

- Cool water, 1/2 cup
- Whole wheat or rye flour, 1 cup
- To feed the starter:
- Cool water (if warm environment) or lukewarm water (if cool environment), 1/2 cup
- All-Purpose Flour Unbleached, 1 cup

DIRECTIONS

1. Day 1: In a one-quart glass container (preferably), combine the flour with cool water. Mix thoroughly, ensuring no dry flour remains. Allow it to rest at room temperature, loosely covered.
2. Day 2: Discard half a cup of the mixture. Add one cup of unbleached flour and half a cup of cool water to the remaining mixture. Mix well and let it rest at room temperature, loosely covered.
3. Day 3: There should be signs of activity, such as bubbling and a fresh aroma. Begin two feedings each day. For each feeding, retain half of the mixture and discard the remainder. Add one cup of all-purpose flour and half a cup of water. Mix well and let it sit at room temperature for 12 hours.
4. Day 4: Keep one cup of the mixture and discard the rest. Add one cup of flour and half a cup of water.
5. Day 5: Repeat the process from day 4. By the end of this day, the starter should be bubbly, doubled in size, and possess a tangy aroma. If it hasn't doubled yet, repeat the process on the 6th and 7th day every 12 hours.
6. Once the starter is ready, give it one final feeding. Discard half of it, mix the remaining half with flour and water, and let it rest at room temperature for 6-8 hours. It should be very bubbly and ready for use. Store it in a jar for long-term use. Feed it once a week with one cup of flour and half a cup of water.

Nutritional Value: 220 kcal, Protein: 3g, Carbs: 36g, Fat: 2g
Note: A sourdough starter is the basis for sourdough bread. It requires regular feeding to stay active and can be kept for a long time with proper maintenance.

2. BASIC SOURDOUGH BREAD

Preparation Time: 10 minutes   **Cooking Time:** 3 hours 5 minutes   **Servings:** 7

INGREDIENTS

- Salt, 1 1/2 tsp
- Active dry yeast, 2 tsp
- Sugar, 1 1/2 tsp
- Lukewarm water, 4-6 tbsp
- Ripe sourdough starter, 2 cups
- All-Purpose Flour (Unbleached), 2 1/2 cups
- Vegetable oil, 2 tbsp

DIRECTIONS

1. Combine all the listed ingredients in the bread machine according to the recommended order provided by the manufacturer.
2. Choose the French bread or long-rise cycle and initiate the baking process.
3. After ten minutes of kneading, assess the dough's consistency and make any necessary adjustments with additional flour or water to achieve a smooth and soft texture.
4. Follow the specific baking instructions outlined by the bread machine manufacturer.
5. Allow the bread to cool thoroughly before slicing it into desired portions.

Nutritional Value: 150 kcal, Protein: 4g, Carbs: 30g, Fat: 2g
Note: Basic Sourdough Bread is a classic and versatile bread made with the tangy flavor of sourdough starter.

3. WHOLE-WHEAT SOURDOUGH BREAD

Preparation Time: 10 minutes   **Cooking Time:** 3 hours 10 minutes   **Servings:** 7

INGREDIENTS

- Vegetable oil, 1 tsp + 1 tbsp
- Sugar, 2 tsp
- Water, 1/2 cup + 3 tbsp
- Whole wheat sourdough starter, 3/4 cup
- Active Dry Yeast, 1 1/2 tsp
- Whole wheat flour, 2 1/4 cups
- Salt, 1 tsp

DIRECTIONS

1. Ensure all ingredients are at ambient temperature, with oil and water at 80°F.
2. Incorporate all ingredients into the bread machine following the recommended order by the manufacturer.
3. Choose the whole wheat setting with a medium crust option. Avoid utilizing the delay function.
4. Monitor the dough consistency during the mixing process and make adjustments with additional water or flour if necessary.
5. Once the bread is fully baked, allow it to cool before slicing.

Nutritional Value: 140 kcal, Protein: 5g, Carbs: 28g, Fat: 1g
Note: Whole-Wheat Sourdough Bread offers the nutritional benefits of whole grains and the distinctive flavor of sourdough.

4. MULTIGRAIN SOURDOUGH BREAD

Preparation Time: 10 minutes   **Cooking Time:** 3 hours 20 minutes   **Servings:** 7

INGREDIENTS

- Sourdough Starter, 3/4 cup
- 7 Grain Cereal (Hot), 2/3 cup
- Butter, 1 1/2 tbsp
- Sea Salt, 3/4 tsp
- Wheat Gluten, 1 tbsp
- Water or Flour (to adjust consistency), 1-2 tbsp
- Packed Brown Sugar, 2 1/2 tbsp
- All-Purpose Flour, 3 cups
- Active Dry Yeast, 1 1/2 tsp
- Water, 2/3 cup

DIRECTIONS

1. Combine all the listed ingredients in the bread machine following the recommended sequence provided by the manufacturer.
2. Choose the basic bread setting with a light crust option. Initiate the baking process.
3. After the bread is finished, allow it to cool before slicing.

Nutritional Value: 180 kcal, Protein: 7g, Carbs: 34g, Fat: 2g
Note: Multigrain Sourdough Bread is packed with wholesome grains and has a hearty texture.

5. FAUX SOURDOUGH BREAD

Preparation Time: 10 minutes   **Cooking Time:** 3 hours 15 minutes   **Servings:** 7

INGREDIENTS

- Salt, 1 1/2 tsp
- Plain yogurt, 1/2 cup
- Lemon juice, 1 tbsp
- Active dry yeast, 2 tsp
- Canola oil, 1 tbsp
- Bread flour, 3 cups
- Water, 3/4 cup

DIRECTIONS

1. Combine all the listed ingredients in the bread machine, following the recommended sequence provided by the manufacturer.
2. Choose either the French or white bread cycle, opting for a light crust. Initiate the baking process by pressing the start button.
3. Allow the bread to cool appropriately before slicing.

Nutritional Value: 160 kcal, Protein: 6g, Carbs: 30g, Fat: 2g
Note: Faux Sourdough Bread mimics the tangy flavor and texture of traditional sourdough bread without requiring a sourdough starter.

6. SOURDOUGH MILK BREAD

Preparation Time: 10 minutes   **Cooking Time:** 3 hours 30 minutes   **Servings:** 7

INGREDIENTS

- Sugar, 4 tbsp
- Bread flour, 4 cups
- Salt, 1 1/4 tsp
- Sour milk or regular milk, 1 1/2 cups
- Active dry yeast, 1 3/4 tsp
- Oil, 1 1/2 tbsp

DIRECTIONS

1. If utilizing buttermilk, create it by adding 1 tbsp of vinegar to 1 cup of milk at room temperature and allowing it to rest for five minutes.
2. Introduce all the ingredients to the bread machine in the recommended sequence according to the manufacturer.
3. Choose the basic setting with a medium crust option. Initiate the process.
4. Assess the dough's consistency after 5-10 minutes of kneading. If it appears excessively dry, include 1 tbsp of water; if it seems excessively moist, incorporate 1 tbsp of flour.
5. Once the bread has finished baking, allow it to cool before slicing.

Nutritional Value: 170 kcal, Protein: 6g, Carbs: 31g, Fat: 2g
Note: Sourdough Milk Bread combines the tangy flavor of sourdough with the softness of milk bread.

7. LEMON SOURDOUGH BREAD

Preparation Time: 10 minutes   **Cooking Time:** 2 hours 25 minutes   **Servings:** 7

INGREDIENTS

- Lemon juice, 2 tsp
- Plain yogurt, 1/3 cup
- Water, 1/2 cup
- Salt, 1 tsp
- Softened butter, 2 tsp
- Regular active dry yeast, 1 3/4 tsp
- Bread flour, 2 cups
- Sugar, 2 tsp

DIRECTIONS

1. Place all the ingredients into the bread machine in the recommended order provided by the manufacturer.
2. Avoid utilizing the delay cycle. Choose either the white bread or French bread setting and initiate the process.
3. After the bread has finished baking, allow it to cool adequately before slicing it into portions.

Nutritional Value: 140 kcal, Protein: 5g, Carbs: 25g, Fat: 2g
Note: Lemon Sourdough Bread adds a refreshing twist to traditional sourdough. The hint of lemon brightens the flavor and makes it perfect for breakfast or as a complement to salads and seafood dishes.

8. SAN FRANCISCO SOURDOUGH BREAD

Preparation Time: 10 minutes   **Cooking Time:** 3 hours 15 minutes   **Servings:** 7

INGREDIENTS

- Lukewarm water, 3/4 cup
- Salt, 2 tsp
- Baking soda, 1/4 tsp
- Room temperature sourdough starter, 1 cup
- Bread flour, 3 cups

Glaze:
- Corn-starch, 1 tsp
- Cold water, 1/2 cup

DIRECTIONS

1. Combine all the ingredients in the bread machine.
2. Choose the basic bread setting with a light crust option. Initiate the baking process.
3. In a small saucepan, mix corn-starch and cold water. Heat the mixture over medium heat, stirring constantly until it thickens.
4. Apply the glaze onto the bread immediately after removing it from the bread machine.
5. Allow the bread to cool completely before slicing.

Nutritional Value: 150 kcal, Protein: 5g, Carbs: 30g, Fat: 1g
Note: San Francisco Sourdough Bread is known for its distinct tangy flavor and chewy texture.

9. SOURDOUGH BEER BREAD

Preparation Time: 10 minutes   **Cooking Time:** 2 hours 30 minutes   **Servings:** 7

INGREDIENTS

- Vegetable oil, 2 tbsp
- Sourdough starter, 1 1/3 cups
- Flat beer, 1/2 cup
- Bread flour, 3 cups
- Salt, 1 1/2 tsp
- Water, 1/4 cup
- Active dry yeast, 1 1/2 tsp
- Sugar, 1 tbsp

DIRECTIONS

1. Combine all the ingredients in the bread machine according to the recommended sequence provided by the manufacturer.
2. Choose the white bread program with a dark crust preference. Initiate the baking process.
3. Allow the bread to cool adequately before slicing it.

Nutritional Value: 150 kcal, Protein: 5g, Carbs: 30g, Fat: 1g
Note: Sourdough Beer Bread combines the unique flavours of sourdough and beer, resulting in a rich and slightly tangy bread.

10. CRUSTY SOURDOUGH BREAD

Preparation Time: 10 minutes **Cooking Time:** 2 hours 25 minutes **Servings:** 7

INGREDIENTS

- Bread flour, 3 cups
- Water, 1/2 cup
- Sourdough starter, 1 cup
- Sugar, 2 tbsp
- Bread machine yeast, 1 tsp
- Salt, 1 1/2 tsp

DIRECTIONS

1. Place all the ingredients in the bread machine following the recommended order provided by the manufacturer.
2. Choose the white cycle with a light crust setting. Initiate the baking process.
3. After the bread is finished, allow it to cool before cutting into slices.

Nutritional Value: 150 kcal, Protein: 5g, Carbs: 30g, Fat: 1g

Note: Crusty Sourdough Bread features a crunchy crust and a soft, tangy interior. It is a versatile bread that can be used for sandwiches or enjoyed with soups and dips.

11. SOURDOUGH CHEDDAR BREAD

Preparation Time: 10 minutes **Cooking Time:** 3 hours 10 minutes **Servings:** 7

INGREDIENTS

- Sourdough starter, 1 cup (at room temperature)
- Salt, 1 1/2 tsp
- Yeast, 1 1/2 tsp
- Warm water, 1/2 cup
- Sugar, 1 1/2 tbsp
- Bread flour, 3 cups
- Grated sharp cheddar cheese, 3/4 cup

DIRECTIONS

1. Combine all ingredients in the bread machine following the recommended sequence provided by the manufacturer.
2. Choose the French bread or white bread setting and initiate the baking process.
3. Allow the bread to cool adequately before slicing it into portions.

Nutritional Value: 180 kcal, Protein: 8g, Carbs: 25g, Fat: 5g

Note: Sourdough Cheddar Bread combines the tangy flavor of sourdough with the richness of cheddar cheese.

12. HERB SOURDOUGH

Preparation Time: 10 minutes **Cooking Time:** 2 hours 55 minutes **Servings:** 7

INGREDIENTS

- Sugar, 3 tbsp
- Water, 3/4 cup
- Salt, 1 1/2 tsp
- Bread flour, 3 to 3 1/2 cups
- Dried parsley, 1 tsp
- Sourdough starter, 1 1/4 cups
- Dried rosemary, 1 1/2 tsp
- Soy margarine, 2 tbsp

DIRECTIONS

1. Place all the ingredients into the bread machine in the recommended order provided by the manufacturer.
2. Begin with 3 cups of flour and assess the consistency of the dough. If necessary, incorporate additional flour, 1 tablespoon at a time, until the dough achieves a smooth and soft texture.
3. Choose the basic cycle with a medium crust setting and initiate the baking process.
4. Once the bread has finished baking, allow it to cool before slicing.

Nutritional Value: 160 kcal, Protein: 5g, Carbs: 30g, Fat: 2g
Note: Herb Sourdough is a flavourful bread infused with dried parsley and rosemary. It adds a delightful aroma and taste to sandwiches or can be enjoyed on its own as a tasty snack.

13. CRANBERRY PECAN SOURDOUGH

Preparation Time: 10 minutes **Cooking Time:** 3 hours 5 minutes **Servings:** 7

INGREDIENTS

- Sweetened dried cranberries, 1 package (3 1/2 oz)
- Water, 2 tbsp + 1 1/4 cup
- Salt, 2 tsp
- Toasted chopped pecans, 3/4 cup
- Bread flour, 4 cups
- Butter, 2 tbsp
- Active dry yeast, 2 tsp
- Non-fat powdered milk, 2 tbsp
- Sugar, 1/4 cup

DIRECTIONS

1. Add all the ingredients to the bread machine following the recommended order provided by the manufacturer.
2. Choose the white bread setting with a medium crust option. Initiate the baking process.
3. Once the bread has finished baking, allow it to cool before slicing.

Nutritional Value: 190 kcal, Protein: 6g, Carbs: 35g, Fat: 3.5g
Note: Cranberry Pecan Sourdough combines the tanginess of cranberries with the crunchiness of pecans.

14. DARK CHOCOLATE SOURDOUGH

Preparation Time: 10 minutes   **Cooking Time:** 2 hours 25 minutes   **Servings:** 7

INGREDIENTS

- Lukewarm water, 3/4 cup
- Cocoa powder, 1/2 cup
- Sourdough starter, 1 cup
- Sugar, 1 tbsp
- Dark chocolate, 1/2 cup (finely diced)
- Oil, 3 tbsp
- Salt, 2 tsp
- Active dry yeast, 1 tbsp
- Bread flour, 3 cups

DIRECTIONS

1. Combine all ingredients in the bread machine following the recommended sequence provided by the manufacturer.
2. Choose the basic cycle with a light crust option. Initiate the process by pressing the start button.
3. Evaluate the consistency of the dough within 5-10 minutes. In case it is excessively moist and adhesive, gradually incorporate one tablespoon of flour until the dough achieves a smooth texture.
4. Once the bread has finished baking, allow it to cool before slicing.

Nutritional Value: 180 kcal, Protein: 6g, Carbs: 32g, Fat: 4g
Note: Dark Chocolate Sourdough is a delightful combination of rich cocoa flavor and the tanginess of sourdough.

4.6: Fruit Bread

1. PINEAPPLE COCONUT BREAD

Preparation Time: 10 minutes   **Cooking Time:** 3 hours 10 minutes   **Servings:** 7

INGREDIENTS

- Pineapple (crushed with juice), 1/2 cup
- Milk, 1/4 cup
- Margarine, 1/4 cup
- Sugar, 1/3 cup
- Coconut extract, 1 tsp
- Egg (beaten), 1
- Mashed banana, 1/2 cup
- All-purpose Flour, 3 cups
- Salt, 1/2 tsp
- Bread machine yeast, 1 1/2 tsp
- Instant potato flakes, 1/2 cup

DIRECTIONS

1. Combine all the ingredients in the bread machine following the recommended sequence provided by the manufacturer.
2. Choose the sweet bread option and select a light crust setting. Initiate the baking process by pressing the start button.
3. Enjoy the bread while it is still freshly prepared.

Nutritional Value: 180 kcal, Protein: 3g, Carbs: 33g, Fat: 4g
Note: Pineapple Coconut Bread is a tropical delight with the sweetness of pineapple and the rich flavor of coconut.

2. BLACK OLIVE BREAD

Preparation Time: 10 minutes   **Cooking Time:** 2 hours 10 minutes   **Servings:** 7

INGREDIENTS

- Warm water, 1 1/2 cups
- Brine (from olives), 1/3 - 1/2 cup
- Bread flour, 3 cups
- Olive oil, 2 tbsp
- Active dry yeast, 2 tsp
- Salt, 1 1/2 tsp
- Whole-wheat flour, 1 2/3 cups
- Sugar, 2 tbsp
- Finely chopped olives, 1/2 - 2/3 cup
- Dried basil, 1 1/2 tsp

DIRECTIONS

1. Mix water with brine.
2. Add all ingredients, except olives, to the bread machine in the suggested order by the manufacturer.
3. Select the wheat or basic setting. Press start.
4. Add the chopped olives at the ingredient signal.
5. Serve fresh bread and brush with olive oil.

Nutritional Value: 170 kcal, Protein: 5g, Carbs: 32g, Fat: 3g
Note: Black Olive Bread is a savoury and aromatic bread with the richness of olives. It pairs well with soups and salads or can be enjoyed on its own.

3. WARM SPICED PUMPKIN BREAD

Preparation Time: 10 minutes **Cooking Time:** 3 hours 10 minutes **Servings:** 7

INGREDIENTS

- White sugar, 1/2 cup
- Canned pumpkin (not pie filling), 1 cup
- Salt, 1/4 tsp
- Brown sugar, 1/2 cup
- Eggs, 2
- Vanilla, 1 tsp
- All-purpose flour, 1 1/2 cups
- Pumpkin pie spice, 1 1/2 tsp
- Chopped walnuts, 1/2 cup
- Canola oil, 1/3 cup
- Baking powder, 2 tsp

DIRECTIONS

1. Coat the bread machine pan with cooking oil.
2. Incorporate all the ingredients into the bread machine according to the manufacturer's recommended order.
3. Choose the Quick cycle with a medium crust setting.
4. Following three minutes, use a spatula to scrape the sides of the pan.
5. Restart the process and serve the bread fresh.

Nutritional Value: 200 kcal, Protein: 4g, Carbs: 26g, Fat: 9g
Note: Warm Spiced Pumpkin Bread is a comforting treat, perfect for the fall season. The aromatic spices and pumpkin flavor make this bread incredibly delicious.

4. ROBUST DATE BREAD

Preparation Time: 10 minutes **Cooking Time:** 2 hours 10 minutes **Servings:** 7

INGREDIENTS

- Boiling water, 3/4 cup
- Unsalted butter (cut into half-inch pieces), 3 tbsp
- Granulated sugar, 2/3 cup
- Baking powder, 1 tsp
- All-purpose flour, 1 1/3 cups
- Vanilla extract, 1 tsp
- Chopped dates, 3/4 cup
- Baking soda, 1 tsp
- Chopped walnuts, 1/3 cup
- Salt, 1/2 tsp

DIRECTIONS

1. Coat the bread machine pan with cooking oil.
2. Incorporate all the ingredients into the bread machine according to the manufacturer's recommended order.
3. Choose the Quick cycle with a medium crust setting.
4. Following three minutes, use a spatula to scrape the sides of the pan.
5. Restart the process and serve the bread fresh.

Nutritional Value: 180 kcal, Protein: 3g, Carbs: 32g, Fat: 5g
Note: Robust Date Bread is a flavourful and moist bread with the natural sweetness of dates and the crunch of walnuts.

5. APPLE SPICE BREAD

Preparation Time: 10 minutes   **Cooking Time:** 3 hours 35 minutes   **Servings:** 7

INGREDIENTS

- Vegetable oil, 1/4 cup
- Milk, 1 cup
- Cinnamon, 1/2 tsp
- Salt, 1 1/2 tsp
- Diced apples (peeled), 1 1/3 cups
- Sugar, 2 tbsp
- Yeast, 2 1/2 tsp
- Bread flour, 3 cups

DIRECTIONS

1. Combine all ingredients, excluding apples, in the bread machine following the recommended order provided by the manufacturer.
2. Choose the medium crust setting and initiate the baking process.
3. Incorporate the apples when prompted during the ingredient signal.
4. Serve the bread while it is still fresh.

Nutritional Value: 180 kcal, Protein: 5g, Carbs: 34g, Fat: 3g
Note: Apple Spice Bread is a delicious and aromatic bread that combines the sweetness of apples with warm spices.

6. LEMON-LIME BLUEBERRY BREAD

Preparation Time: 10 minutes   **Cooking Time:** 3 hours 10 minutes   **Servings:** 7

INGREDIENTS

- Lukewarm heavy cream, 1/4 cup
- Salt, 1 tsp
- Diced butter, 1/3 cup
- Eggs, 3
- All-purpose flour, 1 1/2 cups + 3 tbsp
- Bread flour, 1 1/2 cups
- Blueberries, 1 1/2 cups
- Sugar, 3-4 tbsp + 2 tbsp
- Bread machine yeast, 2 tsp
- Lukewarm water, 1/4 cup
- Lime and lemon juice, 2 tbsp each

DIRECTIONS

1. Place all the listed ingredients, excluding blueberries, into the bread machine according to the recommended order provided by the manufacturer.
2. Choose the basic cycle and select your desired crust setting. Start the bread machine.
3. Add the blueberries when prompted during the ingredient signal.
4. Serve the freshly baked bread with a sprinkle of sugar on top of the loaf.

Nutritional Value: 190 kcal, Protein: 5g, Carbs: 36g, Fat: 3g
Note: Lemon-Lime Blueberry Bread is a tangy and fruity bread with a burst of citrus flavor and juicy blueberries.

7. BANANA WHOLE-WHEAT BREAD

Preparation Time: 10 minutes **Cooking Time:** 3 hours 10 minutes **Servings:** 7

INGREDIENTS

- Egg, 1
- Softened butter, 1 tbsp
- Bread machine yeast, 1 1/2 tsp
- Ripe bananas (mashed), 1/3 cup
- Sugar, 3 tbsp
- Warm water (80 F), 1/4 cup
- Salt, 1/2 tsp
- Bread flour, 1 1/4 cups
- Toasted chopped pecans, 1/3 cup
- Whole wheat flour, 3/4 cup

DIRECTIONS

1. Combine all the listed ingredients, except for nuts, in the bread machine following the recommended order provided by the manufacturer. Include the banana along with the water.
2. Choose the white bread cycle with a light crust setting and initiate the baking process by pressing the start button. Add the nuts when the machine indicates the addition of ingredients. Avoid using the delay feature.
3. Enjoy the freshly baked bread.

Nutritional Value: 190 kcal, Protein: 5g, Carbs: 34g, Fat: 4g
Note: Banana Whole-Wheat Bread is a wholesome and flavourful bread with the natural sweetness of bananas and the nuttiness of pecans.

8. ORANGE CRANBERRY BREAD

Preparation Time: 10 minutes **Cooking Time:** 3 hours 5 minutes **Servings:** 7

INGREDIENTS

- Dried cranberries, 1 cup
- All-purpose flour, 3 cups
- Warm water, 1/2 cup
- Active dry yeast, 2 tsp
- Honey, 3 tbsp
- Plain yogurt, 3/4 cup
- Melted butter, 1 tbsp
- Orange oil, 1 tsp
- Salt, 1 1/2 tsp

DIRECTIONS

1. Combine all the ingredients in the bread machine following the recommended sequence provided by the manufacturer.
2. Choose the basic cycle and set the crust to light. Initiate the bread-making process.
3. Present the freshly baked bread when ready.

Nutritional Value: Calories: 180 kcal, Protein: 4g, Carbs: 36g, Fat: 2g
Note: Orange Cranberry Bread is a delightful combination of citrus and tart flavours.

9. PLUM ORANGE BREAD

Preparation Time: 10 minutes   **Cooking Time:** 3 hours 10 minutes   **Servings:** 7

INGREDIENTS

- Warm water, 1 1/4 cups
- Packed brown sugar, 1/4 cup
- Bread machine yeast, 1 1/2 tsp
- Bread flour, 3 3/4 cups
- Orange juice, 2 tbsp
- Plums, 3/4 cup
- Vegetable oil, 2 tbsp
- Salt, 1 tsp

DIRECTIONS

1. Add all the listed ingredients to the bread machine following the recommended order provided by the manufacturer.
2. Choose the basic cycle and select a medium crust setting.
3. Initiate the bread-making process by pressing the start button, and once ready, savour the delight of freshly baked bread.

Nutritional Value: 170 kcal, Protein: 5g, Carbs: 34g, Fat: 2g
Note: Plum Orange Bread is a delightful combination of sweet plums and tangy orange juice.

10. PEACHES & CREAM BREAD

Preparation Time: 15 minutes   **Cooking Time:** 3 hours 10 minutes   **Servings:** 7

INGREDIENTS

- Egg (beaten), 1
- Salt, 1 1/2 tsp
- Chopped peaches, 1 1/2 cups
- Vegetable oil, 1 1/2 tbsp
- Sugar, 3 tbsp
- Cinnamon, 1/2 tsp
- Bread flour, 3 1/2 cups
- Dry yeast, 2 1/4 tsp
- Heavy cream, 1/4 cup
- Nutmeg, 1/4 tsp
- Rolled oats, 1/2 cup

DIRECTIONS

1. Place all ingredients in the bread machine according to the recommended order provided by the manufacturer.
2. Choose the basic setting and initiate the bread-making process.
3. Indulge in the delightful experience of savoring freshly baked bread.

Nutritional Value: 180 kcal, Protein: 4g, Carbs: 34g, Fat: 3g
Note: Peaches & Cream Bread is a delightful treat with the sweetness of peaches and the richness of cream.

11. FRESH BLUEBERRY BREAD

Preparation Time: 10 minutes **Cooking Time:** 3 hours 10 minutes **Servings:** 7

INGREDIENTS

- Melted butter, 8 tbsp
- Whisked eggs, 2
- Vanilla extract, 1 tsp
- Mashed ripe bananas, 3
- Packed light brown sugar, 1 cup
- All-purpose flour, 2 cups
- Salt, 1/2 tsp
- Baking powder, 2 tsp
- Fresh blueberries, 1 cup

DIRECTIONS

1. Place all the listed ingredients, excluding the blueberries, into the bread machine following the recommended order provided by the manufacturer.
2. Choose the Quick bread cycle and select a light crust setting. Initiate the baking process.
3. Once the initial kneading is complete, incorporate the blueberries.
4. Enjoy the freshly baked bread.

Nutritional Value: 180 kcal, Protein: 3g, Carbs: 35g, Fat: 5g
Note: Fresh Blueberry Bread is a delightful and fruity bread with bursts of juicy blueberries. It's a perfect treat for breakfast or as a snack.

12. BLUEBERRY OATMEAL BREAD

Preparation Time: 10 minutes **Cooking Time:** 3 hours 10 minutes **Servings:** 7

INGREDIENTS

- All-purpose flour, 2 cups
- Quick-cooking oatmeal, 1 cup
- Grated lemon zest, 1 tsp
- Salt, 1/2 tsp
- Baking soda, 1/2 tsp
- Vegetable oil, 1/3 cup
- Baking powder, 2 tsp
- Vanilla extract, 2 tsp
- Sugar, 3/4 cup
- Thawed blueberries, 1 cup
- Skim milk, 1 1/4 cups
- Eggs (lightly whisked), 2

DIRECTIONS

1. Gently coat the defrosted blueberries with flour.
2. Apply a light layer of cooking oil to the bread pan.
3. Combine all ingredients in the bread machine.
4. Choose the quick or cake cycle. Initiate the process.
5. Enjoy the freshly baked bread.

Nutritional Value: 180 kcal, Protein: 4g, Carbs: 32g, Fat: 5g
Note: Blueberry Oatmeal Bread is a wholesome and delicious bread with the goodness of oats and the sweetness of blueberries. It's a perfect choice for breakfast or as a snack.

13. FRAGRANT ORANGE BREAD

Preparation Time: 10 minutes   **Cooking Time:** 3 hours 45 minutes   **Servings:** 7

INGREDIENTS

- Grated orange zest, 1/2 tsp
- Orange juice concentrate, 3 tbsp
- Egg, 1
- Bread flour, 3 cups
- Salt, 1 1/4 tsp
- Water, 1/2 cup + 1 tbsp
- Granulated sugar, 1/4 cup
- Instant dry milk, 2 tbsp
- Softened butter, 1 1/2 tbsp
- Bread machine yeast, 2 tsp
- **For Orange Glaze:**
- Orange juice, 1 tbsp
- Powdered sugar, 3/4 cup

DIRECTIONS

1. Combine all ingredients in the bread machine following the recommended order specified by the manufacturer.
2. Choose the white cycle with a light crust setting. Avoid utilizing the delay feature. Initiate the baking process.
3. In the meantime, Prepare the glaze mixture.
4. Pour the glaze over the freshly baked bread.

Nutritional Value: 180 kcal, Protein: 5g, Carbs: 34g, Fat: 3g
Note: Fragrant Orange Bread is a delightful bread with a burst of citrus flavor. The orange zest and juice concentrate add a vibrant aroma to the bread.

14. MOIST OATMEAL APPLE BREAD

Preparation Time: 10 minutes   **Cooking Time:** 3 hours 10 minutes   **Servings:** 7

INGREDIENTS

- Unsweetened applesauce, 1/3 cup
- Water, 1/3 cup
- Unsweetened apple juice, 2/3 cup
- Honey, 3 tbsp
- Oat bran, 1/4 cup
- Vegetable oil, 2 tbsp
- Quick-cooking oats, 1/3 cup
- Salt, 1 1/2 tsp
- Bread flour, 3 cups
- Bread machine yeast, 2 1/4 tsp

DIRECTIONS

1. Combine all ingredients in the bread machine following the recommended order by the manufacturer.
2. Choose the basic cycle with a light crust option. Initiate the process.
3. Serve the freshly baked bread.

Nutritional Value: 180 kcal, Protein: 4g, Carbs: 33g, Fat: 3g
Note: Moist Oatmeal Apple Bread is a delicious and moist bread with the natural sweetness of apples and the heartiness of oats.

15. STRAWBERRY SHORTCAKE BREAD

Preparation Time: 10 minutes **Cooking Time:** 3 hours 10 minutes **Servings:** 7

INGREDIENTS

- Bread machine yeast, 2 1/2 tsp
- Vanilla extract, 1 tsp
- Warm heavy whipping cream, 1/4 cup
- Bread machine flour, 3 cups
- Warm water, 1/4 cup
- Sugar, 1 tbsp
- Baking powder, 1/8 tsp
- Fresh strawberries, 2 cups + 1/4 cup sugar
- Salt, 1 tsp

DIRECTIONS

1. Pour water and cream into the bread maker's pan, and combine with yeast and sugar. Allow it to rest for 15 minutes.
2. Coat the sliced strawberries with 1/4 cup of sugar.
3. Add all the ingredients to the bread machine in the recommended order provided by the manufacturer.
4. Incorporate the strawberries into the fruit hopper or add them at the designated ingredient signal.
5. Choose the basic cycle with a medium crust setting. Initiate the bread-making process.
6. Slice and serve the freshly baked bread.

Nutritional Value: 190 kcal, Protein: 4g, Carbs: 38g, Fat: 3g
Note: Strawberry Shortcake Bread is a delightful bread that captures the flavours of a classic dessert.

4.7: Grain, Seed, and Nut Breads

1. WHOLE-WHEAT SEED BREAD

Preparation Time: 10 minutes **Cooking Time:** 3 hours 10 minutes **Servings:** 4

INGREDIENTS

- Whole wheat bread flour, 1 1/3 cups
- Water, 1 1/3 cups
- Honey, 3 tbsp
- Salt, 1 tsp
- Softened butter, 2 tbsp
- Flaxseed, 1/2 cup
- Bread flour, 1 1/2 cups
- Sunflower seeds, 1/2 cup
- Active dry yeast, 1 tsp

DIRECTIONS

1. Place all ingredients into the bread machine according to the recommended sequence specified by the manufacturer, excluding the sunflower seeds.
2. Choose the basic cycle on the machine and initiate the process by pressing the start button.
3. When prompted by the kneading cycle notification, incorporate the sunflower seeds.
4. Serve the freshly prepared bread.

Nutritional Value: 132 kcal, Protein: 4g, Carbs: 22g, Fat: 4g
Note: For added crunch and flavor, you can toast the sunflower seeds before adding them to the bread machine.

2. MULTIGRAIN BREAD

Preparation Time: 10 minutes　　**Cooking Time:** 2 hours 40 minutes　　**Servings:** 6

INGREDIENTS

- Multigrain cereal, 3/4 cup
- Softened unsalted butter, 3 tbsp
- Bread flour, 2 1/4 cups
- Warm milk, 1 cup
- Bread machine yeast, 1 tsp
- Packed brown sugar, 1/4 cup
- Salt, 1 tsp

DIRECTIONS

1. Place all ingredients into the bread machine in the recommended sequence according to the manufacturer's instructions.
2. Choose the basic cycle with a light crust setting and initiate the process.
3. Present the bread fresh and ready to enjoy.

Nutritional Value: 172 kcal, Protein: 4g, Carbs: 32g, Fat: 3g
Note: To enhance the nutty flavor, you can toast the multigrain cereal before adding it to the bread machine.

3. TOASTED PECAN BREAD

Preparation Time: 10 minutes　　**Cooking Time:** 3 hours 5 minutes　　**Servings:** 7

INGREDIENTS

- Butter, 2 1/2 tbsp
- Water, 1 1/4 cups
- Old-fashioned oatmeal, 1/2 cup
- Bread flour, 3 cups
- Chopped pecans, 1/2 cup
- Bread machine yeast, 2 tsp
- Dry milk, 2 tbsp
- Sugar, 3 tbsp
- Salt, 1 1/4 tsp

DIRECTIONS

1. Place all the listed ingredients into the bread machine according to the recommended sequence provided by the manufacturer.
2. Choose the appropriate settings for grains and a light crust. Initiate the bread-making process by pressing the start button.
3. Serve the bread while it is still freshly prepared.

Nutritional Value: 190 kcal, Protein: 5g, Carbs: 29g, Fat: 7g
Note: For a richer flavor, you can toast the pecans before adding them to the bread machine.

4. MARKET SEED BREAD

Preparation Time: 10 minutes **Cooking Time:** 3 hours 10 minutes **Servings:** 8

INGREDIENTS

- Olive oil, 2 tbsp
- Tepid water, 1 cup
- Whole wheat bread flour, 1 cup
- Mixed seeds (pumpkin, sunflower, sesame, linseed, & poppy), 1/3 cup
- Salt, 1 tsp
- Dried yeast, 1 1/2 tsp
- Sugar, 1 tbsp
- White bread flour, 2 cups

DIRECTIONS

1. Place all ingredients into the bread machine in the recommended sequence as specified by the manufacturer. Include the seeds as the final addition.
2. Choose the white bread cycle and initiate the process by pressing the start button.
3. Verify the texture of the dough and make adjustments if necessary by gradually adding 1 tbsp of water or flour at a time.
4. Serve the bread while it is fresh and still warm.

Nutritional Value: 158 kcal, Protein: 5g, Carbs: 28g, Fat: 3g
Note: Feel free to customize the mix of seeds according to your preference.

5. CRACKED WHEAT BREAD

Preparation Time: 10 minutes **Cooking Time:** 1 hour 10 minutes **Servings:** 8

INGREDIENTS

- Salt, 1 1/2 tsp
- Bread flour, 2 1/4 cups
- Butter, 1 1/2 tbsp
- Water, 1 1/3 cups
- Honey, 2 tbsp
- Active dry yeast, 2 1/4 tsp
- Whole wheat flour, 1 1/4 cups
- Cracked wheat, 1/2 cup

DIRECTIONS

1. Place all the ingredients into the bread machine's pan, following the recommended order.
2. Choose the basic setting and select your desired crust. Begin the cycle by pressing the start button.
3. Once ready, serve the bread while it's still fresh and savour the delightful taste.

Nutritional Value: 163 kcal, Protein: 5g, Carbs: 31g, Fat: 2g
Note: For added texture and flavour, you can lightly toast the cracked wheat before adding it to the bread machine.

6. DOUBLE COCONUT BREAD

Preparation Time: 10 minutes **Cooking Time:** 4 hours 10 minutes **Servings:** 10

INGREDIENTS

- Egg yolk, 1 only
- Unsweetened coconut milk, 1 cup
- Coconut extract, 1 1/2 tsp
- White flour, 3 cups
- Salt, 3/4 tsp
- Vegetable oil, 1 1/2 tbsp
- Coconut, 1/3 cup
- Bread machine yeast, 1 1/2 tsp
- Sugar, 2 1/2 tbsp

DIRECTIONS

1. Place all ingredients into the bread machine following the recommended order specified by the manufacturer.
2. Choose the sweet cycle option and initiate the process by pressing the start button.
3. Serve the freshly baked bread and savour its delightful taste.

Nutritional Value: 217 kcal, Protein: 4g, Carbs: 33g, Fat: 8g
Note: For an extra coconut flavour, you can toast the shredded coconut before adding it to the bread machine.

7. HONEYED BULGUR BREAD

Preparation Time: 10 minutes **Cooking Time:** 2 hours 10 minutes **Servings:** 12

INGREDIENTS

- Honey, 2 tbsp
- Extra coarse bulgur wheat, 1/4 cup
- Boiling water, 1/4 cup
- Active dry yeast, 1 package
- Salt, 1 tsp
- Bread flour, 1/2 cup
- Vegetable oil, 1 tbsp
- All-purpose flour, 1 1/4 cups
- Water, 3/4 cup
- Skim milk, 1 tbsp

DIRECTIONS

1. Place all ingredients into the bread machine in the recommended order specified by the manufacturer.
2. Choose the basic cycle and initiate the process by pressing the start button.
3. Delight in the delightful freshness of your homemade bread.

Nutritional Value: 156 kcal, Protein: 4g, Carbs: 32g, Fat: 2g
Note: Bulgur wheat adds a hearty texture to the bread. Make sure to use extra coarse bulgur for the best results.

8. FLAXSEED HONEY BREAD

Preparation Time: 10 minutes   **Cooking Time:** 3 hours 40 minutes   **Servings:** 10

INGREDIENTS

- Vegetable oil, 1/4 cup
- Bread flour, 1 1/2 cups
- Honey, 3 tbsp
- Salt, 1 1/2 tsp
- Ground ginger, 1 tsp
- Whole wheat flour, 1 1/2 cups
- Lukewarm water, 1 1/3 cups
- Instant yeast, 1 1/2 tsp
- Ground flaxseed, 1/2 cup

DIRECTIONS

1. Put all the ingredients in the pan of the bread machine following the suggested order.
2. Select the basic cycle and medium crust. Press start.
3. Check the dough's consistency. It should not be too sticky or too dry. Adjust by adding water or flour, one tbsp at a time.
4. Enjoy fresh with butter.

Nutritional Value: 158 kcal, Protein: 5g, Carbs: 27g, Fat: 4g
Note: Flaxseed adds a nutty flavour and extra fiber to the bread. Make sure to use ground flaxseed for better incorporation into the dough.

9. CHIA SESAME BREAD

Preparation Time: 10 minutes   **Cooking Time:** 3 hours 10 minutes   **Servings:** 10

INGREDIENTS

- Organic apple cider vinegar, 1 tbsp
- Olive oil, 1/4 cup
- Salt, 2 tsp
- Almond meal flour, 2/3 cup
- Whisked whole eggs, 3
- Ground sesame seeds, 1 cup
- Gluten-free tapioca flour, 1/2 cup
- Ground chia seeds, 1 cup
- Warm water, 1 cup
- Gluten-free coconut flour, 1/3 cup
- Ground psyllium husks, 3 tbsp

DIRECTIONS

1. In a bowl, add all dry ingredients and sift them together. Remove any large bits.
2. Add all ingredients to the bread machine in the suggested order by the manufacturer.
3. Select the gluten-free cycle and press start.
4. Serve fresh.

Nutritional Value: 146 kcal, Protein: 6g, Carbs: 17g, Fat: 7g
Note: This bread is gluten-free and packed with nutritious chia seeds and sesame seeds. It's a great option for those with gluten sensitivities.

10. QUINOA WHOLE WHEAT BREAD

Preparation Time: 10 minutes   **Cooking Time:** 3 hours 10 minutes   **Servings:** 8

INGREDIENTS

- Honey, 2 tbsp
- Water, 1 1/4 cups
- Olive oil, 1 tbsp
- Salt, 1/2 tsp
- Whole wheat flour, 1 3/4 cups
- Bread flour, 1 3/4 cups
- Toasted sesame oil, a dash
- Uncooked quinoa, 1/3 cup
- Active dry yeast, 1 3/4 tsp

DIRECTIONS

1. Add all ingredients to the bread machine in the suggested order by the manufacturer.
2. Select the basic cycle, light crust. Press start.
3. Serve fresh.

Nutritional Value: 160 kcal, Protein: 5g, Carbs: 28g, Fat: 3g
Note: Toasting the quinoa before adding it to the bread machine can enhance its nutty flavour.

11. PEANUT BUTTER BREAD

Preparation Time: 10 minutes   **Cooking Time:** 3 hours 10 minutes   **Servings:** 9

INGREDIENTS

- Bread flour, 1 1/2 cups
- Peanut butter, 1/2 cup
- Salt, 1/2 tsp
- Whole wheat flour, 1 1/2 cups
- Active dry yeast, 2 1/4 tsp
- Gluten flour, 3 tbsp
- Warm water, 1 1/4 cups
- Brown sugar, 1/4 cup

DIRECTIONS

1. Add all ingredients to the bread machine in the suggested order by the manufacturer.
2. Select the whole wheat setting, light crust. Press start.
3. Serve fresh.

Nutritional Value: 175 kcal, Protein: 7g, Carbs: 28g, Fat: 5g
Note: For a twist, you can add a handful of chopped peanuts to the bread dough.

12. TOASTED HAZELNUT BREAD

Preparation Time: 10 minutes **Cooking Time:** 2 hours 45 minutes **Servings:** 8

INGREDIENTS

- Hazelnut liqueur, 2 tbsp
- All-purpose Flour, 3 cups
- Chopped hazelnuts, 3/4 cup
- Egg, 1
- Sugar, 3 tbsp
- Salt, 3/4 tsp
- Active dry yeast, 1 tsp
- Butter, 3 tbsp
- Milk, 1 cup

For Glaze:
- Milk, 1-2 tsp
- Hazelnut liqueur, 1 tbsp
- Powdered sugar, 1/2 cup

DIRECTIONS

1. Add all ingredients to the bread machine in the suggested order by the manufacturer, except for the nuts.
2. Select the basic setting and light crust. Press start.
3. Add nuts when prompted.
4. Meanwhile, mix all the glaze ingredients. Drizzle over warm bread and serve.

Nutritional Value: 192 kcal, Protein: 6g, Carbs: 26g, Fat: 7g
Note: Toasting the hazelnuts before adding them to the bread machine enhances their flavour.

13. OATMEAL SEED BREAD

Preparation Time: 10 minutes **Cooking Time:** 3 hours 10 minutes **Servings:** 12

INGREDIENTS

- Softened butter, 2 tbsp
- Water, 1 3/4 cups
- Olive oil, 1 tbsp
- Bread flour, 2 cups
- Honey, 1/4 cup
- Quick-cooking oats, 2/3 cup
- Whole wheat flour, 2 cups
- Sunflower seeds, 1/2 cup
- Dry milk, 2 tbsp
- Bread machine yeast, 2 1/2 tsp
- Salt, 1 1/4 tsp

DIRECTIONS

1. Add all ingredients to the bread machine in the suggested order by the manufacturer, except for the sunflower seeds.
2. Select the basic cycle, light crust. Do not use the delay cycle.
3. Press start.
4. Serve fresh.

Nutritional Value: 160 kcal, Protein: 6g, Carbs: 28g, Fat: 4g
Note: For added texture, you can lightly toast the sunflower seeds before adding them to the bread machine.

14. NUTTY WHEAT BREAD

Preparation Time: 10 minutes **Cooking Time:** 3 hours 10 minutes **Servings:** 10

INGREDIENTS

- Unsalted butter, 1 1/2 tbsp
- Buttermilk, 1 1/3 cups
- Maple syrup, 1 1/2 tbsp
- Salt, 1 tsp
- Bread flour, 1 1/4 cups
- Bread machine yeast, 2 1/4 tsp
- Mixed seeds and nuts (pecans, sunflower seeds, pumpkin seeds, and walnuts), 3/4 cup
- Whole wheat flour, 2 1/4 cups

DIRECTIONS

1. Make sure all ingredients are at room temperature.
2. Place all ingredients into the bread machine according to the recommended order provided by the manufacturer, except for the combined seeds and nuts.
3. Choose the whole wheat setting with a light crust option. Initiate the start function.
4. Introduce the seeds and nuts into the mixture when prompted during the cycle.
5. Serve the bread while it is still warm.

Nutritional Value: 194 kcal, Protein: 7g, Carbs: 29g, Fat: 7g
Note: To enhance the flavour of the nuts and seeds, you can lightly toast them before adding them to the bread machine.

15. SUNFLOWER BREAD

Preparation Time: 10 minutes **Cooking Time:** 2 hours 10 minutes **Servings:** 4

INGREDIENTS

- White bread flour, 2 1/2 cups
- Water, 1 1/4 cups
- Dry milk, 2 tbsp
- Sunflower seeds, 1/2 cup
- Salt, 1/2 tsp
- Wheat bread flour, 3/4 cup
- Butter, 2 tbsp
- Fast-rise yeast, 2 tsp
- Honey, 3 tbsp

DIRECTIONS

1. Incorporate all the listed components into the bread machine following the recommended sequence provided by the manufacturer.
2. Select the preferred cycle, including the option to utilize the delay cycle if desired.
3. Initiate the start button and relish the delight of freshly baked bread.

Nutritional Value: 161 kcal, Protein: 6g, Carbs: 28g, Fat: 4g
Note: For added crunch, you can lightly toast the sunflower seeds before adding them to the bread machine.

16. RAISIN SEED BREAD

Preparation Time: 10 minutes **Cooking Time:** 3 hours 10 minutes **Servings:** 6

INGREDIENTS

- Cinnamon, 2 tsp
- Salt, 1/2 tsp
- Whole-wheat flour, 3 cups
- Warm water, 1 cup
- Raisins, 1 cup
- Honey, 4 tbsp
- Mixed seeds (optional), 1 tsp
- Coconut oil, 1/2 cup
- Active dry yeast, 2 tsp

DIRECTIONS

1. Place all ingredients into the bread machine according to the recommended order specified by the manufacturer.
2. Choose the whole-wheat crust option. Initiate the bread-making process.
3. Present the freshly baked bread.

Nutritional Value: 153 kcal, Protein: 4g, Carbs: 31g, Fat: 2g
Note: To enhance the flavour, you can soak the raisins in warm water or rum before adding them to the bread machine.

17. QUINOA OATMEAL BREAD

Preparation Time: 10 minutes **Cooking Time:** 3 hours 50 minutes **Servings:** 8

INGREDIENTS

- Whole wheat flour, 1/2 cup
- Buttermilk, 1 cup
- Bread flour, 1 1/2 cups
- Quick-cooking oats, 1/2 cup
- Bread machine yeast, 1 1/2 tsp
- Water, 2/3 cup
- Honey, 1 tbsp
- Uncooked quinoa, 1/3 cup
- Melted unsalted butter, 4 tbsp
- Salt, 1 tsp
- Sugar, 1 tbsp

DIRECTIONS

1. Cook quinoa in 2/3 cup of water. Allow it to cool.
2. Include all the ingredients, along with the cooled quinoa, into the bread machine following the recommended sequence provided by the manufacturer.
3. Choose the whole grain cycle and initiate the process.
4. Serve the freshly baked bread.

Nutritional Value: 165 kcal, Protein: 6g, Carbs: 29g, Fat: 3g
Note: Quinoa adds protein and a nutty flavour to this bread. Make sure to rinse the quinoa thoroughly before cooking it.

4.8: Herb and Spice Breads

1. OATMEAL-SUNFLOWER BREAD RECIPE

Preparation Time: 10 minutes **Cooking Time:** 4 hours 5 minutes **Servings:** 1

INGREDIENTS

- Milk, 1/2 cup (114 g)
- Water, 1/2 cup (111 g)
- Honey, 1/4 cup (85 g)
- Unsalted butter, 2 tbsp (28 g)
- Salt, 1 1/4 tsp
- Bread flour, 3 cups (360 g)
- Quick or old-fashioned oats, 1/2 cup (50 g)
- Bread machine or instant yeast, 2 and 1/4 tsp
- Hulled sunflower seeds, toasted, 1/2 cup (64 g)

DIRECTIONS

1. Heat the milk and water in the microwave on HIGH for 1 minute.
2. Place the remaining ingredients, excluding the sunflower seeds, into the bread machine pan in the specified order.
3. Initiate the 'Dough' cycle. After 5-10 minutes, assess the consistency of the dough and add 1 tablespoon of extra liquid or flour at a time if necessary. When the dough begins to cling to the sides of the pan, detach it.
4. When the Raisin (Nut) signal sounds or 5-10 minutes before the kneading cycle concludes, incorporate the sunflower seeds. If overlooked, they can still be manually integrated into the dough while Preparationaring the loaf.
5. Once the dough cycle finishes, transfer the dough to a floured surface and shape it into a rectangle. Roll it into a cylinder and position it seam-side down in a greased 9x5-inch loaf pan, tucking the ends underneath.
6. Loosely cover the pan and allow the dough to rise in a warm location until it surpasses the rim of the pan by approximately 1/2 to 1 inch.
7. Preheat the oven to 350°C (175°C).
8. Bake for approximately 30-35 minutes or until the internal temperature exceeds 190°F (88°C).
9. Allow the bread to cool for 5 minutes before removing it from the pan. Then, transfer it to a wire rack to cool completely.
10. Slice and serve the bread while it is still fresh.

Nutritional Value: 128 kcal, Protein: 4g, Carbs: 21g, Fat: 3g
Note: For added texture and flavour, you can lightly toast the sunflower seeds before adding them to the bread machine.

2. BREAD MACHINE - BACON BREAD

Preparation Time: 10 minutes **Cooking Time:** 3 hours 5 minutes **Servings:** 12

INGREDIENTS

- Water, 1 1/3 cups (warm)
- Butter, 4 tbsp (sliced)
- Bread flour, 3 cups
- One Min Oatmeal, 1 cup
- Salt, 1 tsp
- Dark Brown Sugar, 1/4 cup
- Bread Machine Yeast, 1 1/2 tsp
- Bacon Bits, 4 tbsp

DIRECTIONS

1. Configure the Bread Maker for a 2 lb loaf, light crust, and the "standard" bread setting.
2. Introduce all the components, barring the bacon bits, into the bread maker "pan," initiating with the water. Position the yeast in the bread maker, ensuring it avoids contact with the liquid until the device is activated and the components commence merging.
3. Activate the device once you've scrutinized the configurations.
4. Integrate the bacon bits after the bread maker has finished its INITIAL kneading stage. If the bacon pieces become too fragmented and dispersed during the dual kneading stages, you may incorporate them with the remaining components.
5. Lightly scatter some bacon bits atop the dough once the bread maker has finished its LAST kneading stage and prior to the onset of the baking stage.
6. After the bread maker has completed baking, extricate the bread, and lay it on a cooling stand. Utilize protective gloves when withdrawing the bread maker pan, as it will be exceedingly hot.
7. The baking duration is roughly 3 hours for a 2 lb loaf on the light crust and standard bread settings in a Sunbeam bread maker. Nonetheless, baking durations may differ, so heed the "completion" alarm of the bread maker.
8. Once you've input the appropriate configurations, the bread maker will showcase the span of the baking period, permitting you to know when to be in the vicinity to extricate the bread.

Nutritional Value: 182 kcal, Protein: 6g, Carbs: 29g, Fat: 4g
Note: The addition of bacon bits gives this bread a delicious smoky flavour. Make sure to check the manufacturer's instructions for your specific bread machine model, as settings and baking times may vary.

3. BREAD MACHINE LEMON BREAD RECIPE

Preparation Time: 10 minutes **Cooking Time:** 4 hours 15 minutes **Servings:** 1

INGREDIENTS

- Milk, 5/8 cup (150 g)
- Sugar, 1/4 cup (50 g)
- Table salt, 1 tsp (6 g)
- Butter, 1/4 cup (57 g)
- Eggs, 2 large
- Unbleached flour, 3 1/4 cups (390 g)
- Bread machine or instant yeast, 2 1/4 tsp (7 g)
- Melted butter, 1/4 cup (57 g) (for dipping dough pieces)
- Lemon zest of 3 medium lemons & 1 orange mixed
- Sugar, 1/2 cup (100 g)
- Frosting:
- Powdered sugar, 1 cup (227 g)
- Whipping cream, milk, or coffee, 1-2 tbsp (14-28 g)

DIRECTIONS

1. In the bread maker's pan, combine the initial 7 ingredients in the specified sequence. Select the dough cycle. After 5 minutes, lift the lid and inspect the dough. If it sticks to the sides of the pan, gently push it back. If the dough is too firm, add one tablespoon of milk at a time. If it is too warm, incorporate flour one tablespoon at a time.
2. Once the dough cycle completes and the dough has doubled in size, transfer it to a floured surface and roll it out into a rectangular shape, approximately measuring 8 x 10 inches.
3. Utilize a pizza cutter or knife to slice the dough into wide diamond shapes.
4. Dip each diamond into melted butter, and then coat them with a mixture of zest from lemons or oranges combined with sugar.
5. Position the first piece horizontally in a Bundt Pan. Stand the second piece upright against the first one, and continue this arrangement until all the pieces are lined up in the pan. Gently press the final pieces together to seal, aiming for a secure connection without obsessing over perfection.
6. Cover the pan with plastic wrap, a shower cap, or a tea towel, and allow it to rise until it nearly doubles in size in a warm location.
7. Remove the cover and bake the bread for 30-35 minutes in a preheated oven at 350 degrees Fahrenheit (175 degrees Celsius). Around midway through the baking time, lightly place a piece of foil on top to prevent excessive browning.
8. Let the bread cool for 5 minutes before removing it from the pan. Flip it upside down to showcase the crusty top.
9. Combine powdered sugar with the liquid of your choice, and drizzle the mixture over the warm bread.

Nutritional Value: 171 kcal, Protein: 4g, Carbs: 30g, Fat: 4g
Note: The combination of lemon and orange zest gives this bread a refreshing citrus flavour. The frosting can be adjusted by adding more or less liquid to achieve the desired consistency.

4. BREAD MACHINE PIZZA DOUGH WITH VARIATIONS

Preparation Time: 10 minutes **Cooking Time:** 30 minutes **Servings:** 16

INGREDIENTS

- Water, 1 1/2 cups
- Vegetable oil or olive oil, 1 1/2 tbsp
- Bread flour, 3 3/4 cups
- Granulated sugar, 1 tbsp + 1 tsp
- Salt, 1 1/2 tsp
- Active dry yeast, 1 1/2 tsp

DIRECTIONS

1. Place all the ingredients into the bread machine.
2. Retrieve the dough from the machine and flatten it to fit a pizza pan, ensuring a one-inch-thick border.
3. Preheat the oven to 400°F (200°C).
4. Apply a light coating of olive oil or vegetable oil onto the dough, allowing the crust to rise for 10-15 minutes. Subsequently, spread tomato sauce and select your desired toppings.
5. Place the pizza in the oven and bake for a minimum of 20-25 minutes, or until the crust turns golden brown and the cheese has melted.

Nutritional Value: 144 kcal, Protein: 4g, Carbs: 26g, Fat: 2g
Note: This versatile pizza dough recipe can be customized with various toppings to suit your preferences. Get creative and enjoy homemade pizza right from your bread machine.

5. ROASTED GARLIC BREAD FOR THE BREAD MACHINE

Preparation Time: 10 minutes **Cooking Time:** 1 hour 20 minutes **Servings:** 16

INGREDIENTS

- One bulb roasted garlic
- Butter, 3 tbsp
- Garlic, minced, 4 cloves
- Water, 1/2 cup
- Milk, 1/3 cup
- Bread flour, 2-3/4 cups
- Parmesan cheese, grated, 1/3 cup
- Sugar, 2 tbsp
- Salt, 1 tsp
- Garlic powder, 1/2 tsp
- Bread machine yeast, 1-1/2 tsp

DIRECTIONS

1. Gently mash the roasted garlic after separating the cloves. Utilize 1/4 cup for a loaf weighing around 1-1/2 pounds.
2. In a dish suitable for microwave use, combine the minced garlic and butter. Microwave on high until the garlic becomes fragrant, which usually takes about 1-2 minutes.
3. Add all the ingredients, excluding the roasted garlic, to the bread machine pan in the order recommended by the manufacturer.
4. Pay attention to the bread machine's kneading process and add additional warm water if the dough feels stiff or strained. The absorption of flour can differ due to environmental factors and the source of the wheat, so adjusting the liquid content is a common practice when using bread machines.
5. When the Raisin/Nut signal sounds or approximately 5-10 minutes before the final kneading cycle concludes, incorporate the lightly mashed roasted garlic. Choose the Medium or Light Crust Colour option and select the Basic/White cycle.
6. Follow the baking directions provided by the bread machine for baking the bread.
7. Once baked, allow the bread to cool for 5 minutes before removing it from the pan. Invert the loaf so that the crusty top becomes visible.

Nutritional Value: 138 kcal, Protein: 4g, Carbs: 23g, Fat: 3g
Note: The addition of roasted garlic gives this bread a rich and savoury flavour. Roasting the garlic beforehand brings out its sweetness. Enjoy this delicious garlic bread as a side or as the base for sandwiches and bruschetta.

6. BREAD MACHINE GARLIC BASIL BREAD

Preparation Time: 10 minutes   **Cooking Time:** 3 hours 30 minutes   **Servings:** 7

INGREDIENTS

- Warm milk, 2/3 cup
- Warm water, 1/4 cup
- Warm sour cream, 1/4 cup
- Sugar, 1 1/2 tsp
- Butter, softened, 1 tbsp
- Parmesan cheese, 1 tbsp
- Salt, 1 tsp
- Minced garlic, 1/2 tsp
- Dried basil, 1/2 tsp
- Garlic powder, 1/2 tsp
- Active dry yeast, 2-1/4 tsp
- Bread flour, 3 cups

DIRECTIONS

1. Add all the ingredients to the tray of the bread machine following the order recommended by the manufacturer.
2. Choose the Basic setting on your bread machine.
3. Follow the instructions provided with the bread machine for baking.

Nutritional Value: 138 kcal, Protein: 4g, Carbs: 25g, Fat: 2g
Note: This garlic basil bread is flavourful and aromatic. The combination of garlic, basil, and Parmesan cheese creates a delicious savoury bread. Enjoy it as a side, or use it to make flavourful sandwiches and paninis.

7. PEPPER ASIAGO LOAF

Preparation Time: 10 minutes   **Cooking Time:** 3 hours 30 minutes   **Servings:** 16

INGREDIENTS

- Water, 1 cup
- Egg, 1
- Butter, melted, 1 tbsp
- Nonfit dry milk powder, 1/2 cup
- Shredded Asiago cheese, 1/2 cup
- Chopped green onion, 4 1/2 tsp
- Sugar, 1 tbsp
- Salt, 1 1/4 tsp
- Coarsely ground pepper, 1/2 tsp
- Active dry yeast, 2 1/4 tsp
- Bread flour, 3 cups

DIRECTIONS

1. Place all the components in the bread machine tray in the sequence recommended by the manufacturer.
2. Choose the Basic setting for your bread machine.
3. Proceed with the baking process according to the instructions provided by the bread machine's manufacturer.

Nutritional Value: 146 kcal, Protein: 6g, Carbs: 23g, Fat: 4g
Note: The combination of Asiago cheese and coarsely ground pepper gives this bread a rich and spicy flavour. It pairs well with soups, salads, and cheese platters.

8. SPICED RAISIN BREAD

Preparation Time: 10 minutes **Cooking Time:** 3 hours 45 minutes **Servings:** 24

INGREDIENTS

- Water, 1 cup plus 2 tbsp
- Raisins, 3/4 cup
- Butter, softened, 2 tbsp
- Brown sugar, 2 tbsp
- Ground cinnamon, 2 tsp
- Salt, 1 tsp
- Ground nutmeg, 1/4 tsp
- Ground cloves, 1/4 tsp
- Grated orange zest, 1/4 tsp
- Active dry yeast, 2 1/4 tsp
- Bread flour, 3 cups

DIRECTIONS

1. Arrange all the components in the designated compartment of the bread machine, following the sequence recommended by the manufacturer.
2. opt for the Basic setting on your bread machine.
3. Proceed with the baking process as per the provided instructions for the bread machine.

Nutritional Value: 105 kcal, Protein: 2g, Carbs: 21g, Fat: 2g
Note: This spiced raisin bread is perfect for breakfast or as a sweet snack. The combination of spices and raisins adds warmth and sweetness to the bread.

9. MEXICAN BREAD

Preparation Time: 10 minutes **Cooking Time:** 3 hours 25 minutes **Servings:** 16

INGREDIENTS

- Water, 1 cup plus 2 tbsp
- Monterey Jack cheese, 1/2 cup
- Chopped green chilies, 1 can
- Butter, softened, 1 tbsp
- Sugar, 2 tbsp
- Crushed red pepper flakes, 1 to 2 tbsp
- Non-fat dry milk powder, 1 tbsp
- Ground cumin, 1 tbsp
- Salt, 1 1/2 tsp
- Bread flour, 3 1/4 cups
- Active dry yeast, 2 1/2 tsp

DIRECTIONS

1. Put all the ingredients into the designated tray of the bread machine in the sequence recommended by the manufacturer.
2. Choose the Basic setting on your bread machine.
3. Follow the baking instructions provided by the bread machine's manufacturer.

Nutritional Value: 148 kcal, Protein: 5g, Carbs: 25g, Fat: 3g
Notes: This Mexican bread is infused with flavours of cheese, green chilies, and spices. It is perfect for making sandwiches or enjoying it on its own.

10. BREAD MACHINE HERB & PARMESAN BREAD RECIPE

Preparation Time: 10 minutes **Cooking Time:** 3 hours 15 minutes **Servings:** 10

INGREDIENTS

- Lukewarm water, 1 1/3 cups
- Olive oil, 2 tbsp
- Crushed garlic, 2 cloves
- Fresh herbs, 3 tbsp (chopped)
- Bread flour, 4 cups
- Salt, 1 scant tsp
- Sugar, 1 tbsp
- Parmesan cheese, grated, 4 tbsp
- Active dry yeast, 2 1/4 tsp

DIRECTIONS

1. Place all of the ingredients into the bread machine.
2. Choose the Basic setting on your bread machine.
3. Follow the baking instructions provided by the bread machine.

Nutritional Value: 185 kcal, Protein: 6g, Carbs: 34g, Fat: 2g
Note: This herb and Parmesan bread is packed with flavour. The combination of fresh herbs and grated Parmesan cheese gives it a delicious savoury taste. Enjoy it as a side or use it to make sandwiches and bruschetta.

11. ITALIAN HERB BREAD

Preparation Time: 10 minutes **Cooking Time:** 3 hours 5 minutes + cooling **Servings:** 7

INGREDIENTS

- Water (70°-80°), 1 cup
- Butter, 3 tbsp
- Dried basil, 1/2 tsp
- Egg, lightly beaten, 1
- Sugar, 2 tbsp
- Salt, 1 tsp
- Dried tarragon, 1/4 tsp
- Dill weed, 1/4 tsp
- Dried thyme, 1/8 tsp
- Grated Parmesan cheese, 2/3 cup
- Dried oregano, 1 tsp
- Bread flour, 3 cups
- Garlic powder, 1 tsp
- Active dry yeast, 2-1/4 tsp

DIRECTIONS

1. In the bread machine pan, put all the ingredients in the sequence recommended by the manufacturer.
2. Choose the Basic setting for your bread machine.
3. Bake as per the instructions provided by the bread machine.

Nutritional Value: 149 kcal, Protein: 5g, Carbs: 26g, Fat: 3g
Note: This Italian herb bread is infused with the flavours of basil, oregano, and Parmesan cheese. It is perfect for serving with Italian dishes or as a base for garlic bread.

12. PEPPERONI BREAD

Preparation Time: 10 minutes **Cooking Time:** 3 hours 20 minutes **Servings:** 7

INGREDIENTS

- Warm water (70°-80°), 1 cup
- Olive oil, 2 tbsp
- Bread flour, 3 cups
- Sugar, 2 tbsp
- Salt, 1 1/2 tsp
- Garlic powder, 1 tsp
- Italian seasoning, 1 tsp
- Active dry yeast, 2 1/4 tsp
- Sliced pepperoni, 1 cup
- Shredded mozzarella cheese, 1 cup

DIRECTIONS

1. Place all the ingredients, except the pepperoni and mozzarella cheese, in the bread machine pan in the order recommended by the manufacturer.
2. Choose the Basic setting for your bread machine.
3. Once the dough is finished, take it out from the machine and roll it into a rectangular shape.
4. Layer the pepperoni and mozzarella cheese over the dough.
5. Roll up the dough tightly, ensuring the edges are sealed.
6. Grease a loaf pan and place the rolled dough in it. Cover and allow it to rise for approximately 30 minutes.
7. Preheat your oven to 350°F (175°C).
8. Bake the bread for 25-30 minutes or until it turns golden brown. Allow it to cool before slicing and serving.

Nutritional Value: 202 kcal, Protein: 9g, Carbs: 26g, Fat: 7g
Note: This pepperoni bread is a delicious and savoury treat. It's perfect for serving as an appetizer, snack, or party food. Enjoy it warm or at room temperature.

13. SPAGHETTI BREAD

Preparation Time: 10 minutes **Cooking Time:** 3 hours 30 minutes **Servings:** 16

INGREDIENTS

- Warm water (70°-80°), 1 cup
- Olive oil, 2 tbsp
- Bread flour, 3 cups
- Grated Parmesan cheese, 1/3 cup
- Sugar, 1 tbsp
- Garlic powder, 1-2 tsp
- Salt, 1 tsp
- Dried oregano, 1/4 tsp
- Dried savoury, 1/8 tsp
- Dried marjoram, 1/8 tsp
- Dried basil, 1/8 tsp
- Dried thyme, 1/8 tsp
- Rubbed sage, 1/8 tsp
- Crushed dried rosemary, 1/8 tsp
- Active dry yeast, 1 package (1/4 ounce)

DIRECTIONS

1. In the bread machine pan, put all the ingredients in the sequence recommended by the manufacturer.
2. Choose the Basic setting for your bread machine.
3. Cook following the instructions provided by the bread machine.
4. After the bread is finished, allow it to cool before slicing.

Nutritional Value: 142 kcal, Protein: 4g, Carbs: 25g, Fat: 2g
Note: Spaghetti bread is a fun and creative twist on traditional bread. The herbs and Parmesan cheese give it a savoury flavor that pairs well with pasta dishes. It's great for making sandwiches or serving as a side with spaghetti or other Italian meals.

14. MULTIGRAIN SPECIAL BREAD

Preparation Time: 10 minutes **Cooking Time:** 3 hours 30 minutes **Servings:** 7 (2 lbs)

INGREDIENTS

- Water (70°-80°), 1 cup
- Canola oil, 2 tbsp
- Egg yolks, 2
- Active dry yeast, 2-1/4 tsp
- Molasses, 1/4 cup
- Salt, 1 tsp
- Bread flour, 1-1/2 cups
- Rye flour, 1/2 cup
- Whole wheat flour, 1 cup
- Quick-cooking oats, 1/4 cup
- Toasted wheat germ, 1/4 cup
- Cornmeal, 1/4 cup
- Dry milk powder (non-fat), 1/2 cup

DIRECTIONS

1. In the bread machine pan, arrange all the ingredients in the sequence recommended by the manufacturer.
2. Choose the Basic setting on your bread machine.
3. Follow the instructions provided with the bread machine for baking.
4. After the bread is finished, allow it to cool before cutting into slices.

Nutritional Value: 198 kcal, Protein: 7g, Carbs: 36g, Fat: 3g
Note: This multigrain bread is hearty and nutritious, with a combination of different grains and oats. It's perfect for sandwiches or as toast for breakfast. Enjoy it with your favourite spreads or toppings.

15. CRACKED PEPPER BREAD

Preparation Time: 10 minutes **Cooking Time:** 3 hours 10 minutes **Servings:** 16

INGREDIENTS

- Water (70°-80°), 1-1/2 cups
- Olive oil, 3 tbsp
- Sugar, 3 tbsp
- Salt, 2 tsp
- Minced chives, 3 tbsp
- Minced garlic, 2 cloves
- Garlic powder, 1 tsp
- Dried basil, 1 tsp
- Cracked black pepper, 1 tsp
- Grated Parmesan cheese, 1/4 cup
- Bread flour, 4 cups
- Active dry yeast, 2-1/2 tsp

DIRECTIONS

1. In the bread machine pan, arrange all the ingredients following the manufacturer's recommended order.
2. Choose the Basic setting on your bread machine.
3. Follow the instructions provided with your bread machine for the baking process.
4. Allow the bread to cool before slicing it.

Nutritional Value: 150 kcal, Protein: 5g, Carbs: 26g, Fat: 3g
Note: This cracked pepper bread is packed with flavour from the combination of cracked black pepper, garlic, chives, and Parmesan cheese. It's a great accompaniment to soups and salads or enjoyed on its own with your favourite spreads.

16. CARAWAY DILL BREAD

Preparation Time: 5 minutes **Cooking Time:** 3 hours 5 minutes **Servings:** 7

INGREDIENTS

- Water (70°-80°), 2/3 cup
- Butter (softened), 1 tbsp
- Dry milk powder (non-fat), 1 tbsp
- Sugar, 2 tbsp
- Salt, 1 tsp
- Dried parsley flakes, 2 tbsp
- Caraway seeds, 1 tbsp
- Dill weed, 1 tbsp
- Bread flour, 2 cups
- Active dry yeast, 1-1/2 tsp

DIRECTIONS

1. Add all the ingredients to the pan of your bread machine, following the recommended order provided by the manufacturer.
2. Choose the Basic setting on your bread machine.
3. Follow the instructions provided with your bread machine for baking.
4. After the bread is finished baking, allow it to cool before slicing.

Nutritional Value: 92 kcal, Protein: 3g, Carbs: 17g, Fat: 1g
Note: Caraway dill bread is a flavourful and aromatic bread with hints of caraway seeds and dill. It pairs well with soups and stews or can be enjoyed on its own with a spread of butter.

4.9: International Breads

1. ITALIAN PANETTONE

Preparation Time: 10 minutes **Cooking Time:** 3 hours 40 minutes **Servings:** 7

INGREDIENTS

- Rum, 1/2 tsp
- Butter, 2 tbsp
- Whole eggs, 2
- Lemon zest, 1 tsp
- Salt, 1/4 tsp
- Granulated sugar, 1/4 cup
- Orange zest, 1 tsp
- Sultana raisins, 1/4 cup
- Anise seeds, 1/2 tsp
- All-purpose flour, 2 1/2 cups
- Water, 1/2 cup
- Bread machine yeast, 1 1/4 tsp
- Candied orange, finely diced, 2 tbsp
- Citron peel, 2 tbsp
- Toasted slivered almonds, 1/4 cup

DIRECTIONS

1. Combine all ingredients, excluding raisins, peel, and nuts, into the bread machine following the recommended order provided by the manufacturer.
2. Choose the basic bread cycle and initiate the process by pressing the start button.
3. Introduce raisins, candied oranges, citron peel, and almonds at the designated ingredient alert.
4. Prior to the baking cycle commencing, apply a coat of melted butter onto the top of the dough.
5. Allow the bread to bake as per the instructions provided by the bread machine.
6. Indulge in the delightful freshness of homemade panettone bread.

Nutritional Value: 180 kcal, Protein: 4g, Carbs: 32g, Fat: 4g
Note: Panettone is a traditional Italian sweet bread usually enjoyed during the holiday season. It is known for its light and fluffy texture, enriched with flavours of rum, citrus zest, raisins, and nuts.

2. ITALIAN POP BREAD

Preparation Time: 10 minutes   **Cooking Time:** 3 hours 40 minutes   **Servings:** 7

INGREDIENTS

- Water, 1 1/2 cups
- Salt, 1 1/2 tsp
- Bread flour, 4 1/4 cups
- Bread machine yeast, 2 tsp
- Olive oil, 2 tbsp
- Sugar, 2 tbsp

DIRECTIONS

1. Place all ingredients into the bread machine following the recommended order specified by the manufacturer.
2. Choose the basic cycle option and initiate the process by pressing the start button.
3. Permit the bread machine to finish the cycle and bake the bread.
4. When the bread is ready, take it out of the machine and allow it to cool before slicing.

Nutritional Value: 120 kcal, Protein: 4g, Carbs: 22g, Fat: 1g
Note: Italian bread is a classic and versatile loaf that is perfect for sandwiches or served alongside pasta dishes. It has a crisp crust and a soft, airy interior.

3. BREAD OF THE DEAD (PAN DE MUERTOS)

Preparation Time: 10 minutes   **Cooking Time:** 3 hours 40 minutes   **Servings:** 7

INGREDIENTS

- Bread flour, 1 3/4 cups
- Whole eggs, 3
- Butter, 3 tbsp
- Sugar, 1/4 cup
- Salt, 1/2 tsp
- Water, 1/4 cup
- Grated orange peel, 1/4 tsp
- Yeast, 1 tsp
- Anise, 1/8 tsp

DIRECTIONS

1. Place all ingredients into the bread machine according to the recommended order specified by the manufacturer.
2. Choose the sweet bread cycle, ensuring the crust setting is set to light, and initiate the bread-making process.
3. Permit the bread machine to finish the cycle and bake the bread.
4. After completion, take out the bread from the machine and allow it to cool before serving.

Nutritional Value: 130 kcal, Protein: 3g, Carbs: 22g, Fat: 4g
Note: Bread of the Dead, also known as Pan de Muertos, is a traditional Mexican bread often made for the Day of the Dead celebrations. It has a slightly sweet flavour and is typically decorated with bone-shaped pieces on top.

4. MEXICAN SWEET BREAD

Preparation Time: 10 minutes   **Cooking Time:** 3 hours 10 minutes   **Servings:** 7

INGREDIENTS

- Milk, 1 cup
- Bread flour, 3 cups
- Whole egg, 1
- Yeast, 1 1/2 tsp
- Sugar, 1/4 cup
- Salt, 1 tsp
- Butter, 1/4 cup
- Cinnamon, 1/2 tsp

DIRECTIONS

1. Incorporate all the ingredients into the bread machine following the recommended order as specified by the manufacturer.
2. Choose the sweet bread cycle with a light crust setting and initiate the process.
3. Permit the bread machine to finish the cycle and bake the bread.
4. After completion, extract the bread from the machine and allow it to cool before serving.

Nutritional Value: 150 kcal, Protein: 4g, Carbs: 26g, Fat: 3g

Note: Mexican sweet bread, also known as Concha's, is a popular treat in Mexico. It has a soft and slightly sweet dough, often decorated with a crumbly, sugary topping shaped like a seashell. Enjoy this bread with a hot cup of coffee or hot chocolate for a delightful snack or breakfast option.

5. CHALLAH

Preparation Time: 10 minutes   **Cooking Time:** 2 hours 30 minutes   **Servings:** 7

INGREDIENTS

- All-purpose/bread flour, 4 1/4 cups
- Water, 1 1/2 cups
- Salt, 1 1/8 tsp
- Brown sugar, 1/2 cup
- Active dry yeast, 1 tbsp
- Sesame or poppy seed
- Whole egg, lightly whisked, 1
- Egg yolks, 5
- Oil, 1/3 cup

DIRECTIONS

1. Place all ingredients into the bread machine in the recommended order provided by the manufacturer.
2. Choose the dough cycle and initiate the process.
3. Preheat the oven to 350°F (175°C) and carefully take out the dough from the machine.
4. Separate the dough into 2 portions, and then divide each portion into three equal parts.
5. Weave the three elongated pieces together and securely seal the ends.
6. Position the braided dough onto a greased baking sheet, cover it, and allow it to rise for approximately 30 minutes.
7. Prior to baking, apply an egg wash onto the dough and sprinkle sesame or poppy seeds on top. Bake for 30 minutes. Savour the delightful taste of freshly baked challah bread.

Nutritional Value: 150 kcal, Protein: 6g, Carbs: 28g, Fat: 3g

Note: Challah is a traditional Jewish bread typically enjoyed on Sabbath and holidays. It has a rich, slightly sweet flavour and a soft, fluffy texture. Challah is often braided, and it is the golden crust and beautiful appearance make it an inviting addition to any meal or celebration.

6. RUSSIAN BLACK BREAD

Preparation Time: 10 minutes　　**Cooking Time:** 3 hours 40 minutes　　**Servings:** 7

INGREDIENTS

- All-Purpose Flour, 2 1/2 cups
- Dark Rye Flour, 1 1/4 cups
- Cocoa Powder, Unsweetened, 2 tbsp
- Caraway Seeds, 1 tbsp
- Dried Onion Minced, 1/2 tsp
- Instant Crystals Coffee, 1 tsp
- Fennel Seeds, 1/2 tsp
- Dark Molasses, 1 1/2 tbsp
- Active Dry Yeast, 2 tsp
- Water, 1 1/3 cups
- Sea Salt, 1 tsp
- Vegetable Oil, 3 tbsp
- Sugar, 1 tsp
- Vinegar, 1 1/2 tbsp

DIRECTIONS

1. Place all ingredients into the bread machine in the recommended order as specified by the manufacturer.
2. Choose the sweet bread cycle and initiate the baking process.
3. Allow the bread machine to finish the cycle and thoroughly bake the bread.
4. Once completed, take out the bread from the machine and allow it to cool before serving.

Nutritional Value: 110 kcal, Protein: 3g, Carbs: 22g, Fat: 2g
Note: Russian black bread is a hearty and flavourful bread with a dark colour and rich taste. It is often enjoyed with savoury dishes or used to make traditional Russian sandwiches like "smorrebrod." The combination of caraway seeds, molasses, and rye flour gives this bread its distinctive flavour.

7. RUSSIAN RYE BREAD

Preparation Time: 10 minutes　　**Cooking Time:** 3 hours 40 minutes　　**Servings:** 7

INGREDIENTS

- Warm water, 1/2 cup + 2 tbsp
- Melted butter, 1 1/2 tbsp
- Dark honey, 2 tbsp
- Salt, 1 tsp
- Active dry yeast, 1 1/4 tsp
- Rye flour, 3/4 cup
- Bread flour, 1 1/2 cups

DIRECTIONS

1. Incorporate all components into the bread machine according to the recommended sequence specified by the manufacturer.
2. Choose the basic cycle with a medium crust preference and commence the process by pressing the start button.
3. Permit the bread machine to finalize the cycle and carry out the bread-baking procedure.
4. Subsequently, when finished, extract the bread from the machine and allow it to cool before serving.

Nutritional Value: 150 kcal, Protein: 4g, Carbs: 30g, Fat: 2g
Note: Russian rye bread is a dense and flavourful bread with a distinctively tangy taste. It pairs well with savoury toppings like cured meats, pickles, and cheeses. Enjoy it as part of a traditional Russian meal, or use it to make delicious open-faced sandwiches.

8. PORTUGUESE CORN BREAD

Preparation Time: 10 minutes   **Cooking Time:** 4 hours 10 minutes   **Servings:** 7

INGREDIENTS

- Active dry yeast, 1 1/2 tsp
- Yellow cornmeal, 1 cup
- Bread flour, 1 1/2 cups
- Olive oil, 1 tbsp
- Sugar, 2 tsp
- Cold water, 1 1/4 cups
- Salt, 3/4 tsp

DIRECTIONS

1. Mix half of the cornmeal with cold water until well combined. Let it come to room temperature.
2. Add all ingredients to the bread machine in the suggested order by the manufacturer.
3. Select the basic cycle and press start.
4. Allow the bread machine to complete the cycle and bake the bread.
5. Once done, remove the bread from the machine and let it cool before serving.

Nutritional Value: 110 kcal, Protein: 3g, Carbs: 20g, Fat: 2g
Note: Portuguese cornbread, also known as Broa, is a traditional bread made with a combination of cornmeal and wheat flour. It has a slightly dense texture and a sweet flavor. This bread is commonly served alongside soups and stews or enjoyed on its own with butter or cheese.

9. AMISH WHEAT BREAD

Preparation Time: 10 minutes   **Cooking Time:** 3 hours 40 minutes   **Servings:** 7

INGREDIENTS

- Canola Oil, 1/4 cup
- Whole Wheat Flour, 2 3/4 cups
- Warm water, 1.12 cups
- Salt, 1/2 tsp
- Granulated Sugar, 1/3 cup
- Active yeast, 1 package
- Whole egg, 1

DIRECTIONS

1. Add sugar, yeast, and warm water to a bowl and let it rest for 8 minutes.
2. Place all ingredients into the pan of the bread machine in the manufacturer's suggested order.
3. Select the basic bread cycle with a light or dark crust setting and press start.
4. Before the second cycle of kneading starts, switch off the machine and then restart it. This gives the bread two cycles to rise fully.
5. Enjoy fresh bread.

Nutritional Value: 130 kcal, Protein: 4g, Carbs: 23g, Fat: 3g
Note: Amish wheat bread is a simple and wholesome bread made with whole wheat flour. It has a slightly dense texture and a nutty flavor. Enjoy this bread as part of a nutritious breakfast, or use it to make delicious sandwiches.

10. BRITISH HOT CROSS BUNS

Preparation Time: 10 minutes **Cooking Time:** 3 hours 40 minutes **Servings:** 18-24 buns

INGREDIENTS

- Milk, 3/4 cup
- Whole egg + 1 yolk, lightly whisked
- Sugar, 6 tbsp
- Cinnamon, 3/4 tsp
- Butter, 1/3 cup
- Nutmeg, 1/2 tsp
- Yeast, 1 tbsp
- Ground cloves, 1/4 tsp
- Candied fruit, 1/2 cup
- Salt, 3/4 tsp
- Grated lemon rind, 1 1/2 tsp
- Whole wheat Flour, 3 cups
- Lemon juice, 1/2 tsp
- Milk, 1 tbsp
- Icing sugar, 1/2 cup

DIRECTIONS

1. Add all ingredients, except candied fruit, to the bread machine in the manufacturer's suggested order.
2. Select the dough cycle and press start.
3. Preheat the oven to 375°F (190°C) and Preparationare a baking tray by spraying it with oil and placing parchment paper.
4. Take the dough out from the machine and slice it into 18 to 24 pieces.
5. Shape each piece into a ball and place them in the Preparationared baking tray, spacing them half an inch apart.
6. Cover the tray and let the buns rise in a warm place until they double in size.
7. Using a knife, make a cross on top of each bun.
8. Bake in the preheated oven for 12 to 15 minutes.
9. Meanwhile, mix lemon juice, milk, and icing sugar to make the glaze. Drizzle the glaze over the buns and serve.

Nutritional Value: 140 kcal, Protein: 3g, Carbs: 26g, Fat: 3g
Note: British Hot Cross Buns are spiced, and fruity buns traditionally enjoyed on Good Friday. They are marked with a cross symbol on top, representing the crucifixion. These buns have a soft texture and are best served warm with butter or jam.

11. HAWAIIAN BREAD

Preparation Time: 10 minutes **Cooking Time:** 3 hours 10 minutes **Servings:** 7

INGREDIENTS

- Vegetable oil, 2 tbsp
- Dry milk, 2 tbsp
- Honey, 2 1/2 tbsp
- Whole egg, 1
- Fast-rising yeast, 2 tsp
- Pineapple juice, 3/4 cup
- Salt, 3/4 tsp
- Bread flour, 3 cups

DIRECTIONS

1. Add all ingredients to the bread machine in the suggested order by the manufacturer.
2. Select the sweet bread cycle with a light crust setting and press start.
3. Allow the bread machine to complete the cycle and bake the bread.
4. Once done, remove the bread from the machine and let it cool before serving.

Nutritional Value: 150 kcal, Protein: 5g, Carbs: 28g, Fat: 2g
Note: Hawaiian bread, also known as sweet bread, is a soft and slightly sweet bread with a hint of pineapple flavor. It is a popular bread in Hawaii and is often used for making sandwiches and French toast or enjoyed on its own. This bread is perfect for tropical-inspired dishes and adds a touch of sweetness to any meal.

12. GREEK EASTER BREAD

Preparation Time: 10 minutes **Cooking Time:** 2 hours 40 minutes **Servings:** 7

INGREDIENTS

- Caster sugar, 1/2 cup
- Whole eggs, 3
- Dried yeast, 2 tsp
- Baker's flour, 4 1/2 cups
- Mahalepi, 2 tsp
- Butter, 1/2 cup + 1 tbsp, melted
- Milk, 1/3 cup
- Lukewarm water, 1/3 cup
- Grated orange rinds, juice from half an orange

DIRECTIONS

1. Add 1 tbsp of sugar, water, and yeast to the machine's pan. Mix lightly and let it rest for 8 minutes.
2. Add the rest of the ingredients to the pan.
3. Select the dough cycle and press start.
4. Preheat the oven to 338°F (170°C) and Preparationare a baking tray by spraying cooking oil and placing parchment paper.
5. Take the dough out and cut it into three pieces. Roll each piece into a sausage shape and pinch at one end.
6. Braid the dough and pinch the top and bottom to create a circle.
7. Fit three eggs, colored if desired, into the circled dough and let it rest for 20 minutes.
8. Bake in the preheated oven for 20 minutes. Serve.

Nutritional Value: 150 kcal, Protein: 5g, Carbs: 25g, Fat: 4g
Note: Greek Easter bread, also known as Tsoureki, is a traditional bread often enjoyed during Greek Easter celebrations. It has a soft and fluffy texture, enriched with flavours of orange and spices like mahalepi. This bread is often decorated with colored eggs and is a symbol of rebirth and new beginnings.

13. FIJI SWEET POTATO BREAD

Preparation Time: 10 minutes **Cooking Time:** 2 hours 15 minutes **Servings:** 7

INGREDIENTS

- Active dry yeast, 2 tsp
- Mashed sweet potatoes (plain), 1 cup
- Bread flour, 4 cups
- Salt, 1 1/2 tsp
- Water, 2 tbsp + 1/2 cup
- Softened butter, 2 tbsp
- Dark brown sugar, 1/3 cup
- Chopped pecans
- Vanilla extract, 1 tsp
- Dry milk powder, 2 tbsp
- Ground nutmeg, 1/4 tsp
- Ground cinnamon, 1/4 tsp

DIRECTIONS

1. Add all ingredients, except pecans, to the bread machine in the suggested order by the manufacturer.
2. Select the white bread cycle with a light crust setting and press start.
3. Add pecans at the ingredient signal.
4. Allow the bread machine to complete the cycle and bake the bread.
5. Once done, remove the bread from the machine and let it cool before serving.

Nutritional Value: 140 kcal, Protein: 4g, Carbs: 26g, Fat: 3g
Note: Fiji Sweet Potato Bread is a unique and flavourful bread made with mashed sweet potatoes. It has a slightly sweet taste and a moist texture.

14. ZA'ATAR BREAD

Preparation Time: 10 minutes   **Cooking Time:** 3 hours 40 minutes   **Servings:** 7

INGREDIENTS

- Bread flour, 3 1/2 cups
- Water, 1 1/3 cups
- Sugar, 1 1/4 tsp
- Olive oil, 2 1/2 tbsp
- Quick yeast, 2 tsp
- Salt, 1 tsp
- Za'atar, 2 1/2 tsp

DIRECTIONS

1. Add all ingredients to the bread machine in the suggested order by the manufacturer.
2. Select the quick bread cycle with a medium crust setting and press start.

Nutritional Value: 140 kcal, Protein: 4g, Carbs: 27g, Fat: 2g
Note: Za'atar bread is a Middle Eastern bread infused with the flavours of za'atar spice blend, which typically includes thyme, sumac, sesame seeds, and other herbs. It has a unique and aromatic taste. Enjoy this bread on its own, or use it as a base for delicious sandwiches or dips.

4.10: Sweet Breads

1. CHOCOLATE CHIP PEANUT BUTTER BANANA BREAD

Preparation Time: 10 minutes   **Cooking Time:** 3 hours 10 minutes   **Servings:** 7

INGREDIENTS

- Eggs, 3
- Butter (softened), 1/2 cup
- Mashed bananas (very ripe), 1 1/2 cups
- Sugar, 1 1/4 cups
- Vegetable oil, 1/2 cup
- All-purpose flour, 1 1/2 cups
- Salt, 1 tsp
- Plain Greek yogurt, 1/2 cup
- Vanilla, 1 tsp
- Peanut butter + chocolate chips, 1 cup
- Baking soda, 1 tsp

DIRECTIONS

1. Combine all ingredients, excluding chocolate chips and nuts, into the bread machine following the recommended sequence provided by the manufacturer.
2. Choose the batter bread cycle and initiate the process.
3. Incorporate the chocolate chips and nuts when prompted, and remove the paddle. Savour the delight of freshly baked bread.

Nutritional Value: 220 kcal, Protein: 5g, Carbs: 28g, Fat: 11g
Note: Chocolate Chip Peanut Butter Banana Bread is a delicious and indulgent bread that combines the flavours of chocolate, peanut butter, and ripe bananas. It's perfect as a sweet treat or a special breakfast. Enjoy it fresh or toasted with a spread of butter or peanut butter.

2. CHOCOLATE SOUR CREAM BREAD

Preparation Time: 10 minutes   **Cooking Time:** 3 hours 40 minutes   **Servings:** 7

INGREDIENTS

- Bread Flour, 3 3/4 cups
- Butter, 3 tbsp
- Sour cream, 3/4 cup
- Yeast, 2 1/4 tsp
- Sugar, 1 tbsp
- Water, 3/4 cup
- Chocolate chips
- Salt, 1 tsp

DIRECTIONS

1. Add all the ingredients to the bread machine following the recommended sequence as provided by the manufacturer.
2. Choose the basic cycle with a light crust option and initiate the process.
3. Enjoy the freshly baked bread.

Nutritional Value: 180 kcal, Protein: 4g, Carbs: 27g, Fat: 6g
Note: Chocolate Sour Cream Bread is a rich and moist bread with a delightful chocolate flavor. The addition of sour cream adds a tangy and creamy texture.

3. NECTARINE COBBLER BREAD

Preparation Time: 10 minutes   **Cooking Time:** 3 hours 40 minutes   **Servings:** 7

INGREDIENTS

- Active dry yeast, 1 package
- Bread flour, 2 1/2 cups
- Salt, 1 tsp
- Nutmeg, 1/4 tsp
- Nectarine, 1 cup
- Gluten flour, 1 tbsp
- Packed brown sugar, 1/4 cup
- Cinnamon, 1/4 tsp
- Peach juice, 1/3 cup
- Whole wheat flour, 1/2 cup
- Cinnamon, 1/4 tsp
- Vanilla extract, 1 tsp
- Dried peaches, 1/3 cup, chopped
- Sour cream, 1/3 cup
- Butter, 1 tbsp
- Baking soda, 1/8 tsp

DIRECTIONS

1. Ensure that all ingredients are at room temperature.
2. Place all ingredients into the bread machine in the recommended sequence as provided by the manufacturer.
3. Choose the sweet bread cycle and initiate the process.
4. Delight in the delectable aroma and relish the pleasure of freshly baked bread.

Nutritional Value: 160 kcal, Protein: 4g, Carbs: 29g, Fat: 3g
Note: Nectarine Cobbler Bread is a fruity and aromatic bread with the flavours of nectarines and cinnamon. It's reminiscent of a warm and comforting cobbler dessert. Enjoy this bread on its own or toasted with a spread of butter or cream cheese.

4. SOUR CREAM MAPLE BREAD

Preparation Time: 10 minutes **Cooking Time:** 3 hours 10 minutes **Servings:** 7

INGREDIENTS

- Melted butter, 1/2 cup
- All-purpose flour, 2 1/2 cups
- Baking soda, 1/2 tsp
- Sugar, 1/2 cup
- Baking powder, 1 tsp
- Salt, 1/2 tsp
- Mashed ripe bananas, 2 cups
- Maple syrup, 4 tsp
- Nutmeg, 2 tsp
- Sour cream, 1/4 cup
- Walnuts or pecans, 1/3 cup
- Vanilla, 1 tsp
- Raisins, 1/3 cup
- Whisked eggs, 2

DIRECTIONS

1. Combine all the listed ingredients, excluding raisins and walnuts, into the bread machine following the recommended order provided by the manufacturer.
2. Choose the cake cycle on the machine and initiate the process.
3. Introduce the walnuts once the ingredient signal is given.
4. Enjoy the freshly baked bread.

Nutritional Value: 200 kcal, Protein: 4g, Carbs: 32g, Fat: 7g
Note: Sour Cream Maple Bread is a moist and flavourful bread with a hint of maple sweetness. The sour cream adds richness and moisture, while the walnuts or pecans provide a delightful crunch. Enjoy this bread as a dessert or a special treat with a cup of coffee or tea.

5. BARMBRACK BREAD

Preparation Time: 10 minutes **Cooking Time:** 3 hours 10 minutes **Servings:** 7

INGREDIENTS

- Bread flour, 2 cups
- Coin enclosed in foil
- Salt, 1/2 tsp
- Golden raisins, 1/2 cup
- Ground allspice, 1/2 tsp
- Active dry yeast, 1 1/2 tsp
- Sugar, 1/4 cup
- Orange zest, 2 tbsp
- Currants, 1/2 cup
- Non-fat powdered milk, 2 tbsp
- Softened butter, 2 tbsp
- Water, 3/4 cup + 2 tbsp

DIRECTIONS

1. Place all the listed ingredients into the bread machine, excluding the coin, currants, and raisins, following the recommended order provided by the manufacturer.
2. Choose the basic cycle with a medium crust setting and initiate the baking process.
3. When the ingredient signal indicates, incorporate the raisins and currants. Apply a generous amount of spray oil to the foil-covered coin.
4. Ten minutes before the baking cycle commences, carefully position the coin beneath the surface of the bread dough. Allow the bread to bake thoroughly.

Nutritional Value: 180 kcal, Protein: 5g, Carbs: 35g, Fat: 3g
Note: Barmbrack Bread is a traditional Irish fruit bread often enjoyed during Halloween. It is known for containing hidden objects, like a coin, which symbolizes luck or wealth.

6. APPLE BUTTER BREAD

Preparation Time: 10 minutes   **Cooking Time:** 4 hours 10 minutes   **Servings:** 7

INGREDIENTS

- Apple butter, 1/2 cup
- Water, 1 cup
- Sugar, 1 tbsp
- Vegetable oil, 2 tbsp
- Whole wheat flour, 1 cup
- Bread flour, 2 cups
- Active dry yeast, 1 1/2 tsp
- Salt, 1 tsp

DIRECTIONS

1. Add all ingredients to the bread machine in the suggested order by the manufacturer.
2. Select the sweet cycle and press start.
3. Adjust dough consistency by adding 1 tbsp of flour if too sticky and 1 tbsp of water if too dry.
4. Enjoy fresh bread.

Nutritional Value: 170 kcal, Protein: 4g, Carbs: 31g, Fat: 3g
Note: Apple Butter Bread is a moist and flavourful bread with the sweetness and aroma of apple butter. It's perfect for a cosy breakfast or a delicious snack. Enjoy this bread on its own or spread with apple butter for an extra burst of apple flavor.

7. CRUSTY HONEY BREAD

Preparation Time: 10 minutes   **Cooking Time:** 3 hours 10 minutes   **Servings:** 7

INGREDIENTS

- Sugar, 1 tsp
- Honey, 1 tbsp
- Warm water, 1 1/8 cup
- Olive oil, 1 tbsp
- Bread machine yeast, 1 package
- Salt, 1 tsp
- Bread flour, 3 cups

DIRECTIONS

1. Add all ingredients to the bread machine in the suggested order by the manufacturer.
2. Select the white bread cycle with a medium crust setting and press start.
3. Enjoy fresh bread.

Nutritional Value: 160 kcal, Protein: 4g, Carbs: 31g, Fat: 2g
Note: Crusty Honey Bread is a classic bread with a touch of sweetness from honey and a crusty exterior. It's perfect for sandwiches or enjoyed with a hearty soup. Slice it thick or thin, and savour the delightful flavor and texture.

8. HONEY GRANOLA BREAD

Preparation Time: 10 minutes **Cooking Time:** 3 hours 10 minutes **Servings:** 7

INGREDIENTS

- Butter, 2 tbsp
- Water, 1 1/4 cups
- Bread flour, 3 cups
- Granola cereal, 3/4 cup
- Honey, 4 tbsp
- Bread machine yeast, 1 1/2 tsp
- Dry milk, 2 tbsp
- Salt, 1 tsp

DIRECTIONS

1. Add all ingredients to the bread machine in the suggested order by the manufacturer.
2. Select the basic cycle with a light or medium crust setting and press start.

Nutritional Value: 190 kcal, Protein: 5g, Carbs: 37g, Fat: 3g
Note: Honey Granola Bread is a hearty and wholesome bread with the added crunch and sweetness of granola. It's perfect for breakfast or as a healthy snack. Enjoy this bread toasted and topped with your favourite spreads or simply on its own.

9. BLACK BREAD

Preparation Time: 10 minutes **Cooking Time:** 4 hours 15 minutes **Servings:** 7

INGREDIENTS

- Applesauce, 2 2/3 tbsp
- Water, 1 1/3 cups
- Salt, 1 tsp
- Coffee granules, 1 tsp (instant)
- Cider vinegar, 1 1/2 tbsp
- Dried onion flakes, 1 tsp
- All-purpose flour, 2 cups
- Active dry yeast, 2 1/2 tsp
- Fennel seed, 1/4 tsp
- Dark molasses, 1 1/3 tbsp
- Rye flour, 1 1/3 cups
- Caraway seeds, 2 1/2 tsp
- Oat bran, 2/3 cup
- Sugar, 1 tsp
- Cocoa powder (unsweetened), 2 tbsp

DIRECTIONS

1. Add all ingredients to the bread machine in the suggested order by the manufacturer.
2. Select the basic cycle and press start.
3. Serve fresh bread.

Nutritional Value: 160 kcal, Protein: 5g, Carbs: 31g, Fat: 2g
Note: Black Bread is a dense and flavourful bread with a deep, dark colour. It's often associated with European cuisine and pairs well with savoury dishes like soups and stews. Enjoy this unique bread for its rich taste and texture.

10. APPLE CIDER BREAD

Preparation Time: 10 minutes **Cooking Time:** 3 hours 40 minutes **Servings:** 7

INGREDIENTS

- Apple cider (80°F), 1 1/4 cup
- Butter (softened), 2 tbsp
- Active dry yeast, 2 1/4 tsp
- White bread flour, 3 cups
- Ground cinnamon, 1 tsp
- Salt, 1 tsp
- Packed brown sugar, 2 tbsp

DIRECTIONS

1. Place all ingredients into the bread machine in the suggested order by the manufacturer.
2. Select the basic cycle with a light crust setting and press start.
3. Enjoy fresh bread.

Nutritional Value: 180 kcal, Protein: 4g, Carbs: 34g, Fat: 3g
Note: Apple Cider Bread is a deliciously spiced bread with the subtle sweetness of apple cider. It's perfect for the fall and winter seasons when apple flavours are in abundance. Enjoy this bread toasted with butter or apple butter for a comforting treat.

11. COFFEE CAKE

Preparation Time: 10 minutes **Cooking Time:** 3 hours 15 minutes **Servings:** 7

INGREDIENTS

- Salt, 1 1/2 tsp
- Raisins, 3/4 cup
- Strong brewed coffee (70°-80°F), 1 cup
- Canola oil, 3 tbsp
- Bread flour, 3 cups + 1 tbsp
- Egg (lightly beaten), 1
- Ground cloves, 1/4 tsp
- Ground cinnamon, 1 tsp
- Ground allspice, 1/4 tsp
- Sugar, 3 tbsp
- Active dry yeast, 2 1/2 tsp

DIRECTIONS

1. Coat raisins with 1 tbsp of flour and set it aside.
2. Add all ingredients, except raisins, to the bread machine in the suggested order by the manufacturer.
3. Select the basic cycle with your desired crust colour and press start.
4. Add raisins at the ingredient signal.
5. Serve fresh bread.

Nutritional Value: 180 kcal, Protein: 4g, Carbs: 35g, Fat: 3g
Note: Coffee Cake is a delightful and aromatic bread with the flavours of coffee and warm spices. It's perfect for breakfast or as a sweet treat with a cup of coffee or tea. Enjoy this bread with or without a glaze for added sweetness.

12. PUMPKIN COCONUT BREAD

Preparation Time: 10 minutes **Cooking Time:** 4 hours 10 minutes **Servings:** 7

INGREDIENTS

- Coconut extract, 1 1/2 tsp
- Pumpkin puree, 1/2 cup
- Egg yolk (only), 1
- Coconut milk (unsweetened), 1/2 cup
- Olive oil, 1 1/2 tbsp
- Coconut, 1/3 cup
- Bread machine yeast, 1 1/2 tsp
- Sugar, 2 1/2 tbsp
- Regular flour, 3 cups
- Salt, 3/4 tsp

DIRECTIONS

1. Place all ingredients into the bread machine in the suggested order by the manufacturer.
2. Select the sweet bread cycle with your desired crust setting and press start.
3. Enjoy fresh bread.

Nutritional Value: 160 kcal, Protein: 4g, Carbs: 29g, Fat: 3g
Note: Pumpkin Coconut Bread combines the warm flavours of pumpkin and the tropical taste of coconut. It's a delightful bread with a moist and tender texture. Enjoy this bread as a seasonal treat or whenever you crave the comforting flavours of pumpkin and coconut.

13. VANILLA ALMOND MILK BREAD

Preparation Time: 10 minutes **Cooking Time:** 3 hours 40 minutes **Servings:** 7

INGREDIENTS

- Olive oil, 2 tbsp
- Honey, 2 tbsp
- Whole wheat flour, 2 cups
- Active dry yeast, 2 1/4 tsp
- Bread flour, 1 1/4 cups
- Vanilla almond milk, 1 1/4 cups
- Vital gluten, 1 tbsp
- Salt, 1 1/2 tsp

DIRECTIONS

1. Add all ingredients to the bread machine in the suggested order by the manufacturer.
2. Select the wheat bread cycle with a light crust setting and press start.
3. Enjoy.

Nutritional Value: 160 kcal, Protein: 6g, Carbs: 29g, Fat: 2g
Note: Vanilla Almond Milk Bread is a fragrant and flavourful bread with a hint of vanilla and the nutty taste of almond milk. It's perfect for toasting or making sandwiches. Enjoy this bread with your favourite spreads or fillings.

14. TRIPLE CHOCOLATE BREAD

Preparation Time: 10 minutes **Cooking Time:** 3 hours 40 minutes **Servings:** 7

INGREDIENTS

- Vanilla extract, 1 tsp
- Bread flour, 2 cups
- Brown sugar, 2 tbsp
- Margarine or butter, 1 tbsp
- Milk, 2/3 cup
- Active dry yeast, 1 tsp
- Unsweetened cocoa, 1 tbsp
- Salt, 1/2 tsp
- Egg, 1
- Semisweet chocolate chips, 1/2 cup

DIRECTIONS

1. Add all ingredients to the bread machine in the suggested order by the manufacturer.
2. Select the basic cycle and press start.
3. Enjoy fresh bread.

Nutritional Value: 180 kcal, Protein: 6g, Carbs: 30g, Fat: 5g
Note: Triple Chocolate Bread is a decadent treat for chocolate lovers. It's loaded with chocolate flavor from cocoa powder and chocolate chips. Enjoy this bread as a dessert or a special indulgence. Serve it warm or toasted with a drizzle of chocolate sauce for extra sweetness.

15. CHOCOLATE OATMEAL BANANA BREAD

Preparation Time: 10 minutes **Cooking Time:** 3 hours 40 minutes **Servings:** 7

INGREDIENTS

- Milk, 1 oz
- Bananas (mashed), 2
- Butter (melted), 1/3 cup
- Bread flour, 2 cups
- Eggs, 2
- Salt, 1/2 tsp
- Sugar, 2/3 cup
- Baking powder, 1 1/4 tsp
- Chocolate chips, 1/2 cup
- Baking soda, 1/2 tsp
- Walnuts (chopped), 1/2 cup

DIRECTIONS

1. Add all ingredients to the bread machine in the suggested order by the manufacturer.
2. Select the quick bread cycle and press start.
3. Enjoy fresh bread.

Nutritional Value: 180 kcal, Protein: 4g, Carbs: 28g, Fat: 6g
Note: Chocolate Oatmeal Banana Bread is a delightful combination of chocolate, oats, and ripe bananas. It's a moist and flavourful bread that makes for a delicious breakfast or snack. Enjoy this bread on its own or with a spread of butter or Nutella.

4.11: Holiday Breads

1. PANETTONE BREAD

Preparation Time: 10 minutes **Cooking Time:** 3 hours 10 minutes **Servings:** 7

INGREDIENTS

- Vanilla extract, 1 1/2 tsp
- Water, 3/4 cup
- Eggs (whisked), 2
- All-purpose flour, 3 1/4 cups
- Sugar, 2 tbsp
- Butter (softened), 1/4 cup
- Salt, 1 1/2 tsp
- Mixed dried fruit (chopped), 1/2 cup
- Powdered milk, 2 tbsp
- Yeast, 2 tsp

DIRECTIONS

1. Add all ingredients, except dried fruits, to the bread machine in the manufacturer's suggested order.
2. Select the sweet bread cycle with a light crust setting and press start.
3. Enjoy fresh bread.

Nutritional Value: 160 kcal, Protein: 5g, Carbs: 30g, Fat: 2g
Note: Panettone Bread is a traditional Italian Christmas bread filled with dried fruits. It has a light and fluffy texture, and the sweetness of the fruits adds a delightful flavor. Enjoy this bread as a festive treat during the holiday season.

2. WHITE CHOCOLATE CRANBERRY BREAD

Preparation Time: 10 minutes **Cooking Time:** 3 hours 10 minutes **Servings:** 7

INGREDIENTS

- Butter (softened), 4 tsp
- Milk, 1 cup
- Water, 3 tbsp
- Vanilla extract, 1 1/2 tsp
- Egg, 1
- Bread flour, 4 cups
- White baking bar (chopped), 6 tbsp
- Dried cranberries, 1/2 cup
- Sugar, 2 tbsp
- Bread machine yeast, 1 1/4 tsp
- Salt, 1 tsp

DIRECTIONS

1. Add all ingredients, except cranberries, to the bread machine in the suggested order by the manufacturer.
2. Select the white bread cycle with a light crust setting and press start.
3. Add cranberries at the ingredient signal.
4. Enjoy fresh bread.

Nutritional Value: 170 kcal, Protein: 5g, Carbs: 31g, Fat: 3g
Note: White Chocolate Cranberry Bread is a delightful combination of creamy white chocolate and tart cranberries. The bread has a tender crumb and a subtle sweetness. Enjoy this bread as a holiday treat, or anytime you crave a delicious combination of flavours.

3. EGGNOG BREAD

Preparation Time: 10 minutes **Cooking Time:** 3 hours 10 minutes **Servings:** 7

INGREDIENTS

- Salt, 1 1/4 tsp
- Bread flour, 4 cups
- Dried cranberries or raisins, 1/2 cup
- Oil, 1 tbsp
- Milk, 1/2 cup
- Sugar, 2 tbsp
- Eggnog, 1 cup
- Active dry yeast, 1 3/4 tsp
- Cinnamon, 1 tsp

DIRECTIONS

1. Add all ingredients to the bread machine in the suggested order by the manufacturer.
2. Select the basic cycle with a medium crust setting and press start.
3. Enjoy fresh bread.

Nutritional Value: 160 kcal, Protein: 4g, Carbs: 29g, Fat: 3g
Note: Eggnog Bread is a festive and flavourful bread with the rich and creamy taste of eggnog. It's perfect for the holiday season or whenever you want to indulge in the flavours of eggnog. Enjoy this bread toasted with a spread of butter for a delightful treat.

4. WHOLE-WHEAT CHALLAH

Preparation Time: 10 minutes   **Cooking Time:** 3 hours 10 minutes   **Servings:** 7

INGREDIENTS

- Eggs, 2
- Warm water, 1 cup
- Honey, 1/4 or 1/2 cup
- Salt, 1/2 tsp
- Canola oil, 1/4 tsp
- Instant yeast, 2 1/2 tsp
- Whole wheat flour, 4 cups
- White flour, 1 cup

DIRECTIONS

1. Add all ingredients to the bread machine in the suggested order by the manufacturer.
2. Select the dough cycle and press start.
3. Take the dough out on a floured, clean surface and separate it into three long pieces.
4. Braid the dough together and place it on a baking sheet.
5. Brush with egg wash and sprinkle with seeds.
6. Bake at 350°F for 30 minutes or until the bread sounds hollow when tapped.
7. Enjoy fresh bread.

Nutritional Value: 140 kcal, Protein: 5g, Carbs: 27g, Fat: 2g
Note: Whole-Wheat Challah is a traditional Jewish braided bread that is soft and slightly sweet. This healthier version incorporates whole wheat flour for added nutrition. Enjoy this bread on special occasions or as a tasty addition to any meal.

5. PORTUGUESE SWEET BREAD

Preparation Time: 10 minutes   **Cooking Time:** 3 hours 10 minutes   **Servings:** 7

INGREDIENTS

- Egg (whisked), 1
- Sugar, 1/3 cup
- Salt, 3/4 tsp
- Yeast, 2 1/2 tsp
- Milk, 1 cup
- Margarine, 2 tbsp
- Bread flour, 3 cups

DIRECTIONS

1. Add all ingredients to the bread machine in the suggested order by the manufacturer.
2. Select the sweet bread cycle and press start.
3. Serve fresh bread.

Nutritional Value: 150 kcal, Protein: 5g, Carbs: 28g, Fat: 2g
Note: Portuguese Sweet Bread is a traditional bread from Portugal that is soft, slightly sweet, and perfect for breakfast or as a snack. Enjoy this bread on its own or with a spread of butter or your favourite jam.

6. PECAN MAPLE BREAD

Preparation Time: 10 minutes **Cooking Time:** 3 hours 10 minutes **Servings:** 7

INGREDIENTS

- Wholemeal flour, 1 1/4 cups
- Maple syrup, 3 tbsp
- Yeast, 3/4 tsp
- White flour, 1 1/4 cups
- Pecan pieces, 1/2 cup
- Salt, 1 tsp
- Water, 1 cup + 3 tbsp
- Butter, 1 tbsp

DIRECTIONS

1. Add all ingredients, except pecans, to the bread machine in the manufacturer's suggested order.
2. Select the basic cycle with a light crust setting and press start.
3. Enjoy fresh bread.

Nutritional Value: 170 kcal, Protein: 4g, Carbs: 27g, Fat: 6g
Note: Pecan Maple Bread is a flavourful bread with the nutty taste of pecans and the sweetness of maple syrup. It's perfect for breakfast or as a delicious snack. Enjoy this bread toasted or as the base for a tasty sandwich.

7. NANA'S GINGERBREAD

Preparation Time: 10 minutes **Cooking Time:** 3 hours 10 minutes **Servings:** 7

INGREDIENTS

- Melted butter, 3 tbsp
- Rye flour, 3/4 cup
- Milk, 1 1/4 cup
- Grated nutmeg, 1/4 tsp
- Salt, 1 1/2 tsp
- Ground cinnamon, 3/4 tsp
- Bread flour, 2 2/3 cups
- Ground cloves, 1/4 tsp
- Ground ginger, 2 tsp
- Active dry yeast, 2 1/4 tsp
- Brown sugar, 6 tbsp

DIRECTIONS

1. Add milk to a pot, simmer it, and mix with brown sugar and butter.
2. Add the rest of the ingredients to the bread machine in the suggested order by the manufacturer.
3. Select the basic cycle and press start.
4. Serve fresh bread.

Nutritional Value: 160 kcal, Protein: 5g, Carbs: 30g, Fat: 2g
Note: Nana's Gingerbread is a classic recipe passed down through generations. This bread has the warming flavours of ginger, cinnamon, and cloves, making it a perfect treat for the holiday season or any time you crave a comforting slice of bread.

8. BREAD MACHINE BRIOCHE

Preparation Time: 10 minutes **Cooking Time:** 3 hours 10 minutes **Servings:** 7

INGREDIENTS

- Bread flour, 1 3/4 cups
- Active dry yeast, 1 3/4 tsp
- Sugar, 3 tbsp
- Eggs + yolk, 2 + 1
- Water, 1/4 cup
- Unsalted butter, 8 tbsp
- Salt, 3/4 tsp
- Water, 2 tbsp

DIRECTIONS

1. Place all ingredients in the pan of the bread machine, except for butter, in the manufacturer's suggested order.
2. Select the basic cycle with a light crust setting and press start.
3. Dice butter into small pieces.
4. After the end of the kneading cycle or after ten minutes, add butter, one tbsp at a time.
5. Serve fresh bread.

Nutritional Value: 170 kcal, Protein: 5g, Carbs: 21g, Fat: 8g
Note: Bread Machine Brioche is a rich buttery bread that is perfect for indulgent breakfasts or special occasions. Enjoy this bread on its own or use it to make delicious French toast or sandwiches.

9. TRADITIONAL PASCHA

Preparation Time: 10 minutes **Cooking Time:** 3 hours 10 minutes **Servings:** 7

INGREDIENTS

- Warm water, 1/2 cup
- Lemon zest, 1/4
- Fresh lemon juice, 1 tsp
- Orange zest, 1/4
- Warm milk, 1/2 cup
- Fresh orange juice, 1 tsp
- Whole eggs + yolk, 2 + 1
- Vanilla extract, 1/4 tsp
- Anise seed, 1 tsp
- Granulated sugar, 1/3 cup
- Bread flour, 3 1/2 cups
- Salt, 1 tsp
- Active dry yeast, 1 1/2 tsp
- Butter (room temp), 1/2 cup

DIRECTIONS

1. Add all ingredients, except anise seeds, to the bread machine in the manufacturer's suggested order.
2. Select the sweet bread cycle with a dark crust setting and press start.
3. Add seeds at the ingredient signal.
4. Enjoy fresh bread.

Nutritional Value: 180 kcal, Protein: 6g, Carbs: 29g, Fat: 5g
Note: Traditional Paska is a Ukrainian Easter bread that is rich and slightly sweet. It is often decorated with symbols and enjoyed as a special treat during the holiday. Serve this bread with butter or use it as a base for French toast.

10. RAISIN & NUT PASKA

Preparation Time: 10 minutes   **Cooking Time:** 4 hours 5 minutes   **Servings:** 7

INGREDIENTS

- Yeast, 1 package
- Sugar, 3 tbsp
- Water, 1/4 cup
- Cooled melted butter, 4 tbsp
- Salt, 1 1/2 tsp
- Milk, 3/4 cup
- Whole eggs, 2
- Golden raisins, 1/3 cup
- Bread flour, 3 cups
- Honey, 1/4 cup
- Mixed nuts, 3/4 cup
- Regular raisins, 1/3 cup

DIRECTIONS

1. Add all ingredients to the bread machine in the suggested order by the manufacturer.
2. Select the basic cycle and press start.
3. Enjoy fresh bread.

Nutritional Value: 190 kcal, Protein: 6g, Carbs: 33g, Fat: 4g
Note: Raisin & Nut Paska is a festive bread filled with raisins and nuts. It's perfect for Easter or any special occasion. The combination of raisins and nuts adds a delightful texture and flavor to this bread.

11. HONEY CAKE

Preparation Time: 10 minutes   **Cooking Time:** 3 hours 10 minutes   **Servings:** 7

INGREDIENTS

- Milk, 1-2 tbsp
- Honey, 2 tbsp + 1 tsp
- Pancake mix, 1 1/4 cup
- Whole eggs (whisked), 2
- Unsalted butter (room temperature), 1/4 cup + 3 tbsp

DIRECTIONS

1. Dice the butter into 1 cm pieces.
2. Add all ingredients to the bread machine in the suggested order by the manufacturer.
3. Select the cake cycle and press start.
4. At the ingredient signal, scrape the pan with a rubber spatula and let the cycle continue.
5. Serve fresh bread.

Nutritional Value: 180 kcal, Protein: 4g, Carbs: 31g, Fat: 4g
Note: Honey Cake is a moist and flavourful cake-like bread with the natural sweetness of honey. It's perfect for tea time or as a dessert. Enjoy a slice of this delicious bread with a cup of hot tea or coffee.

12. CHRISTMAS FRUIT BREAD

Preparation Time: 10 minutes   **Cooking Time:** 3 hours 10 minutes   **Servings:** 7

INGREDIENTS

- Sugar, 1 1/2 tbsp
- Whole egg, 1
- Bread machine yeast, 1 tsp
- Ground cardamom, 1/2 tsp
- Salt, 1 tsp
- Water, 1 cup + 2 tbsp
- Mixed candied fruit, 1/3 cup
- Softened butter, 1/4 cup
- Bread flour, 3 cups
- Raisins, 1/3 cup

DIRECTIONS

1. Add all ingredients, except the candied fruits and raisins, to the bread machine in the manufacturer's suggested order.
2. Select the basic cycle with a medium crust setting and press start.
3. Add candied fruits and raisins at the ingredient signal.
4. Enjoy fresh bread.

Nutritional Value: 170 kcal, Protein: 4g, Carbs: 34g, Fat: 2g
Note: Christmas Fruit Bread is a festive bread filled with candied fruits and raisins. It's perfect for holiday celebrations or as a special treat. Enjoy this bread with a cup of hot cocoa or as a base for French toast.

13. STOLLEN BREAD

Preparation Time: 10 minutes   **Cooking Time:** 3 hours 10 minutes   **Servings:** 7

INGREDIENTS

- Whole eggs, 2
- Non-fat milk powder, 1/4 cup
- Bread machine yeast, 2 tsp
- Water, 1 cup
- Bread flour, 3 3/4 cups
- Sugar, 2 tbsp
- Lemon zest, 2 tsp
- Butter, 2 tbsp
- Salt, 1 1/2 tsp
- Ground nutmeg, 3/4 tsp
- Slivered almonds (cut into slices), 1/4 cup
- Mixed candied fruit, 1/2 cup
- Raisins, 1/2 cup

DIRECTIONS

1. Add all ingredients, except for raisins, some almond slices, and candied fruits, to the bread machine in the manufacturer's suggested order.
2. Select the basic cycle with a light crust setting and press start.
3. Add raisins and candied fruit at the ingredient signal.
4. Before the baking cycle begins, add the remaining almond slices to the loaf.
5. Enjoy fresh bread.

Nutritional Value: 190 kcal, Protein: 5g, Carbs: 34g, Fat: 4g
Note: Stollen Bread is a traditional German Christmas bread with a rich and sweet flavor. It is typically filled with raisins, candied fruits, and nuts and dusted with powdered sugar. Enjoy this bread as a holiday treat, or gift it to friends and family.

14. JULEKAKE

Preparation Time: 10 minutes   **Cooking Time:** 3 hours 10 minutes   **Servings:** 7

INGREDIENTS

- Bread machine yeast, 1 tsp
- Ground cardamom, 1/2 tsp
- Salt, 1 tsp
- Egg mixed with water to make 1 cup + 2 tbsp
- Sugar, 1 tbsp + 1 tsp
- Mixed candied fruit, 1/3 cup
- Softened butter, 1/4 cup
- Bread flour, 3 cups
- Raisins, 1/3 cup

DIRECTIONS

1. Add all ingredients, except candied fruits and raisins, to the bread machine in the manufacturer's suggested order.
2. Select the white bread cycle with a medium or light crust setting and press start.
3. Add candied fruit and raisins at the nut signal.
4. Enjoy fresh bread.

Nutritional Value: 170 kcal, Protein: 4g, Carbs: 33g, Fat: 3g
Note: Julekake is a Norwegian Christmas bread filled with candied fruits and raisins. It has a soft and slightly sweet flavor, making it a perfect addition to holiday celebrations. Enjoy this bread toasted or with a spread of butter.

15. SPIKED EGGNOG BREAD

Preparation Time: 10 minutes   **Cooking Time:** 3 hours 10 minutes   **Servings:** 7

INGREDIENTS

- Bread flour, 3 cups
- Yeast, 1 1/4 tsp
- Salt, 3/4 tsp
- Eggnog, 1/2 cup
- Milk, 1/4 cup
- Whole egg, 1
- Sugar, 2 tbsp
- Glace cherries (cut into halves), 1/2 cup
- Butter (diced), 2 tbsp
- Nutmeg, 1/2 tsp

DIRECTIONS

1. Place all ingredients in the bread machine, except cherries, in the suggested order by the manufacturer.
2. Select the basic cycle with a medium crust setting and press start.
3. Add cherries at the ingredient signal.
4. Serve fresh bread.

Nutritional Value: 160 kcal, Protein: 5g, Carbs: 30g, Fat: 3g
Note: Spiked Eggnog Bread captures the flavours of the holiday season with the richness of eggnog and a hint of nutmeg. Enjoy this bread as a festive treat or as a delightful addition to a holiday brunch.

16. HOT BUTTERED RUM BREAD

Preparation Time: 10 minutes **Cooking Time:** 3 hours 40 minutes **Servings:** 7

INGREDIENTS

- Rum extract, 1 tbsp
- Whole egg, 1
- Softened butter, 3 tbsp
- Bread flour, 3 cups
- Salt, 1 1/4 tsp
- Ground cinnamon, 1/4 tsp
- Bread machine yeast, 1 tsp
- Ground nutmeg, 1/4 tsp
- Brown sugar (packed), 3 tbsp
- Nut Topping:
- Packed brown sugar, 1 1/2 tsp
- Pecans (finely chopped), 1 1/2 tsp
- Egg yolk (beaten), 1

DIRECTIONS

1. Mix the whole egg with water to make one cup and place it in the bread machine.
2. Add the rest of the ingredients to the bread machine in the suggested order by the manufacturer.
3. Select the sweet cycle with a light or medium crust setting. Do not use the delay feature.
4. Press start.
5. Meanwhile, mix all ingredients of the nut topping in a bowl.
6. Before the baking cycle begins, brush the topping on the loaf.
7. Enjoy fresh bread.

Nutritional Value: 180 kcal, Protein: 5g, Carbs: 32g, Fat: 4g
Note: Hot Buttered Rum Bread is a deliciously spiced bread that captures the flavours of hot buttered rum, a classic winter drink. Enjoy this bread as a cosy treat during cold days or as a delightful addition to holiday gatherings.

4.12: Gluten-Free Breads

1. GLUTEN-FREE WHITE BREAD

Preparation Time: 10 minutes **Cooking Time:** 3 hours 40 minutes **Servings:** 7

INGREDIENTS

- Milk, 1 1/3 cup
- Eggs (whisked), 2
- Vinegar, 1 tsp
- Oil, 6 tbsp
- Gluten-free flour, 450 g
- Quick yeast, 2 tsp
- Salt, 1 tsp
- Sugar, 2 tbsp

DIRECTIONS

1. Mix the milk with vinegar and oil.
2. Add all ingredients to the bread machine in the suggested order by the manufacturer.
3. Select the basic rapid or gluten-free cycle. Press start.
4. Enjoy fresh bread.

Nutritional Value: 180 kcal, Protein: 5g, Carbs: 31g, Fat: 4
Notes: Gluten-Free White Bread is a delicious and versatile bread made with gluten-free flour. It is perfect for those with gluten sensitivities or dietary restrictions. Enjoy this bread toasted or use it to make sandwiches or French toast.

2. BROWN RICE BREAD

Preparation Time: 10 minutes **Cooking Time:** 3 hours 40 minutes **Servings:** 7

INGREDIENTS

- Rice flour, 4 cups
- Cooked brown rice, 1/2 cup
- Salt, 1 1/2 tsp
- Warm water (110°F), 1 1/4 cups
- Bread machine yeast, 2 1/4 tsp
- Sugar, 1 tsp

DIRECTIONS

1. Place all ingredients into the bread machine in the suggested order by the manufacturer.
2. Select the basic cycle with a medium crust setting and press start.
3. Enjoy fresh bread.

Nutritional Value: 160 kcal, Protein: 4g, Carbs: 34g, Fat: 1g

Note: Brown Rice Bread is a hearty and nutritious bread made with the goodness of brown rice. It has a slightly nutty flavor and is perfect for sandwiches or toast. Enjoy this gluten-free option as part of a healthy diet.

3. BROWN RICE & CRANBERRY BREAD

Preparation Time: 10 minutes **Cooking Time:** 3 hours 40 minutes **Servings:** 7

INGREDIENTS

- Non-fat milk powder, 1/4 cup
- Liquid honey, 2 tbsp
- Black pepper, 1/8 tsp
- Water, 1 1/4 cups
- Olive oil, 1 tbsp
- Gluten-free flour, 3 cups
- Cooked brown rice, 3/4 cup
- Salt, 1 1/4 tsp
- Dried cranberries, 2/3 cup
- Pine nuts, 1/4 cup
- Celery seeds, 3/4 tsp
- Bread machine yeast, 1 tsp

DIRECTIONS

1. Add all ingredients, except cranberries, to the bread machine in the suggested order by the manufacturer.
2. Select the basic cycle with a crust setting of your liking. Press start.
3. Add cranberries as the signal ingredient.
4. Enjoy fresh bread.

Nutritional Value: 180 kcal, Protein: 5g, Carbs: 32g, Fat: 4g

Note: Brown Rice & Cranberry Bread combines the earthiness of brown rice with the sweetness of dried cranberries. It's a delightful combination that adds texture and flavor to this gluten-free bread. Enjoy this bread as a healthy and tasty option.

4. GLUTEN-FREE PEASANT BREAD

Preparation Time: 10 minutes   **Cooking Time:** 3 hours 40 minutes   **Servings:** 7

INGREDIENTS

- Vegetable oil, 1 1/2 tbsp
- Xanthan gum, 2 tsp
- Warm water, 1 1/2 cups
- Cider vinegar, 1 tsp
- Gluten-free baking flour, 2 1/2 cups
- Active dry yeast, 1 tbsp
- Salt, 1 tsp
- Eggs, 2
- White sugar, 1 tbsp

DIRECTIONS

1. Place all ingredients into the bread machine in the suggested order by the manufacturer.
2. Select the basic cycle with a light crust setting. Press start.
3. Enjoy fresh bread.

Nutritional Value: 160 kcal, Protein: 4g, Carbs: 32g, Fat: 3g
Note: Gluten-Free Peasant Bread is a simple and hearty bread that is perfect for those following a gluten-free diet. It has a soft texture and a mild flavor, making it versatile for various toppings or spreads. Enjoy this bread as a tasty gluten-free option.

5. GLUTEN-FREE HAWAIIAN LOAF

Preparation Time: 10 minutes   **Cooking Time:** 3 hours 40 minutes   **Servings:** 7

INGREDIENTS

- Oil, 3 tbsp
- Honey, 3 1/2 tbsp
- Eggs, 2
- Pineapple juice (room temperature), 1 cup
- Gluten-free Flour, 4 cups
- Skim dry milk, 3 tbsp
- Fast-rising yeast, 1 tbsp

DIRECTIONS

1. Add all ingredients to the bread machine in the suggested order by the manufacturer.
2. Select the gluten-free cycle with a dark crust setting. Press start.
3. Enjoy fresh bread.

Nutritional Value: 160 kcal, Protein: 4g, Carbs: 32g, Fat: 3g
Note: Gluten-Free Hawaiian Loaf is a tropical-inspired bread with the sweetness of pineapple and honey. It's a delightful gluten-free option that can be enjoyed on its own or used to make delicious sandwiches or toast. Enjoy the taste of the islands with this flavourful bread.

6. VEGAN GLUTEN-FREE BREAD

Preparation Time: 10 minutes **Cooking Time:** 1 hour 45 minutes **Servings:** 7

INGREDIENTS

- Xanthan gum, 1 1/2 tsp
- Olive oil, 2 tbsp
- Gluten-free flour blend, 2 1/4 cups
- Ground flax seeds, 1 tbsp
- Warm water, 1 2/3 cups
- Easy Bake yeast, 2 1/4 tsp
- Sea salt, 1 tsp

DIRECTIONS

1. Add all ingredients to the bread machine in the suggested order by the manufacturer.
2. Select a gluten-free cycle and press start.
3. Before the baking cycle begins, brush olive oil on the loaf and sprinkle seeds.
4. Enjoy fresh bread.

Nutritional Value: 150 kcal, Protein: 3g, Carbs: 27g, Fat: 4g
Note: Vegan Gluten-Free Bread is a plant-based and gluten-free option that is perfect for individuals with dietary restrictions or preferences. It is made with a blend of gluten-free flour and has a soft texture and mild flavor.

4.13: Creative Combination Bread

1. ZUCCHINI PECAN BREAD

Preparation Time: 10 minutes **Cooking Time:** 1 hour 40 minutes **Servings:** 7

INGREDIENTS

- Vegetable oil, 1/3 cup
- Baking powder, 2 tsp
- Eggs (whisked), 3
- Sugar, 3/4 cup
- Baking soda, 1 tsp
- Allspice, 1/2 tsp
- Salt, 1/2 tsp
- Toasted pecans (finely chopped), 1/2 cup
- All-purpose flour, 2 cups
- Cinnamon, 1 tsp
- Zucchini (shredded), 1 cup

DIRECTIONS

1. Add oil and whisked eggs to the bread machine.
2. Add flour, then add the rest of the ingredients, except for zucchini.
3. Select the cake/quick cycle. Dark crust if you like. Press start.
4. Add in the zucchini at the ingredient signal. Serve fresh.

Nutritional Value: 180 kcal, Protein: 4g, Carbs: 28g, Fat: 7g
Note: Zucchini Pecan Bread is a moist and flavourful bread packed with the goodness of zucchini and the crunch of pecans. It's a great way to use up surplus zucchini from your garden.

2. RAISIN BRAN BREAD

Preparation Time: 10 minutes **Cooking Time:** 3 hours 10 minutes **Servings:** 7

INGREDIENTS

- Softened butter, 2 tbsp
- Active dry yeast, 2 1/4 tsp
- Packed brown sugar, 1/4 cup
- Raisin bran, 1 1/2 cups
- Salt, 1/2 tsp
- Lukewarm water, 1 cup + 1 tbsp
- Baking soda, 1/4 tsp
- Raisins, 1/2 cup
- Bread flour, 2 1/4 cups

DIRECTIONS

1. Add all ingredients to the bread machine, except for raisins, in the manufacturer's suggested order.
2. Select the basic bread cycle. Crust colour to your liking.
3. Check the dough if it needs more water or flour; add one tbsp at a time.
4. At the signal, add raisins.
5. Serve fresh bread.

Nutritional Value: 160 kcal, Protein: 4g, Carbs: 33g, Fat: 2g
Note: Raisin Bran Bread is a wholesome and nutritious bread that combines the sweetness of raisins with the goodness of bran. It's perfect for breakfast or as a snack. Enjoy this bread toasted or with your favourite spreads.

3. LEMON POPPY SEED BREAD

Preparation Time: 10 minutes **Cooking Time:** 3 hours 10 minutes **Servings:** 7

INGREDIENTS

- Bread flour, 3 cups
- Dry milk, 1 1/2 tbsp
- Water, 3/4 cup
- Salt, 1 tsp
- Butter, 1 1/2 tbsp
- Honey, 2 tbsp
- Lemon extract, 2 tsp
- Lemon yogurt, 3/4 cup
- Toasted almonds (sliced), 1/2 cup
- Lemon peel, 1 tbsp
- Yeast, 2 tsp
- Poppy seeds, 3 tbsp

DIRECTIONS

1. Add all ingredients to the bread machine in the suggested order by the manufacturer.
2. Select the sweet bread cycle and press start.
3. Enjoy fresh bread.

Nutritional Value: 180 kcal, Protein: 6g, Carbs: 30g, Fat: 4g
Note: Lemon Poppy Seed Bread is a delightful and citrusy bread with a subtle crunch from poppy seeds and a hint of nuttiness from toasted almonds. It's perfect for a refreshing treat or a light breakfast.

4. MUSTARD RYE BREAD

Preparation Time: 10 minutes **Cooking Time:** 3 hours 10 minutes **Servings:** 7

INGREDIENTS

- Ground mustard, 1/4 cup
- Butter, 1 tbsp
- Water, 1 1/4 cups
- Gluten flour, 2 tbsp
- Bread flour, 2 cups
- Rye flour, 1 1/2 cups
- Salt, 3/4 tsp
- Brown sugar, 1 tbsp
- Dry yeast, 1 tsp
- Caraway seed, 1 tsp

DIRECTIONS

1. Add all ingredients to the bread machine in the suggested order by the manufacturer.
2. Select the whole wheat/basic cycle.
3. Serve fresh bread.

Nutritional Value: 170 kcal, Protein: 6g, Carbs: 30g, Fat: 3g
Note: Mustard Rye Bread is a flavourful and hearty bread with a hint of tanginess from ground mustard. It pairs well with deli meats and cheese or makes delicious sandwiches. Enjoy the unique flavor combination of mustard and rye in this bread.

5. HAM & CHEESE BREAD

Preparation Time: 10 minutes **Cooking Time:** 3 hours 10 minutes **Servings:** 7

INGREDIENTS

- Softened butter, 2 tbsp
- Lukewarm water, 1 1/3 cups
- Non-fat dry milk powder, 1 tbsp
- Active dry yeast, 1 tbsp
- Mashed potato flakes, 3 tbsp
- Cornmeal, 2 tbsp
- Salt, 1 1/2 tsp
- Swiss cheese (diced), 1/2 cup
- Bread flour, 4 cups
- Cooked diced ham, 1/2 cup

DIRECTIONS

1. Add all ingredients to the bread machine in the suggested order by the manufacturer.
2. Select the basic bread cycle with a light crust colour. Press start.
3. Enjoy fresh bread.

Nutritional Value: 170 kcal, Protein: 8g, Carbs: 28g, Fat: 3g
Note: Ham & Cheese Bread is a savoury and satisfying bread loaded with diced ham and Swiss cheese. It's perfect for making sandwiches or enjoyed on its own. Indulge in the delicious combination of flavours in every bite.

6. SAUSAGE HERB BREAD

Preparation Time: 10 minutes   **Cooking Time:** 3 hours 10 minutes   **Servings:** 7

INGREDIENTS

- Basil leaves, 3/4 tsp
- Sugar, 1 1/2 tbsp
- Onion (minced), 1 small
- Yeast, 2 1/4 tsp
- Thyme leaves, 3/4 tsp
- Rosemary leaves, 3/4 tsp
- Wheat bran, 3/8 cup
- Salt, 1/2 tbsp
- Italian sausage (crumbled), 6 oz
- Bread flour, 3 cups
- Oregano leaves, 3/4 tsp
- Grated Parmesan, 1 1/2 tbsp
- Warm water, 1 1/8 cup

DIRECTIONS

1. Cook crumbled sausage for three minutes on medium flame. Add onion and cook for five minutes, until the onion softens.
2. Turn off the heat and let it cool. All the ingredients must be at room temperature.
3. Add all ingredients to the bread machine in the suggested order by the manufacturer.
4. Select the white bread cycle and press start. In humid, hot weather, use less water.
5. Serve fresh bread.

Nutritional Value: 190 kcal, Protein: 7g, Carbs: 29g, Fat: 5g
Note: Sausage Herb Bread is a savoury and aromatic bread infused with the flavours of Italian sausage, herbs, and Parmesan cheese. It's perfect for serving alongside soups or enjoyed on its own. Savour the delicious combination of ingredients in every slice.

7. WILD RICE HAZELNUT BREAD

Preparation Time: 10 minutes   **Cooking Time:** 3 hours 10 minutes   **Servings:** 7

INGREDIENTS

- Water, 1 1/4 cups
- Bread flour, 3 cups
- Non-fat milk powder, 1/4 cup
- Liquid honey, 2 tbsp
- Salt, 1 1/4 tsp
- Olive oil, 1 tbsp
- Cooked wild rice, 3/4 cup
- Yeast, 1 tsp
- Pine nuts, 1/4 cup
- Celery seeds, 3/4 tsp
- Hazelnuts, 2/3 cup
- Black pepper, 1/8 tsp

DIRECTIONS

1. Add all ingredients to the bread machine, except cranberries, in the suggested order by the manufacturer.
2. Select the basic cycle with a light crust. Press start.
3. Add cranberries at the ingredient signal.
4. Serve fresh bread.

Nutritional Value: 170 kcal, Protein: 6g, Carbs: 28g, Fat: 4g
Note: Wild Rice Hazelnut Bread is a flavourful and nutty bread with the added texture and taste of cooked wild rice and toasted hazelnuts. It's a unique bread that pairs well with savoury dishes or makes a delicious sandwich. Enjoy the combination of wild rice and hazelnuts in every bite.

8. SPINACH FETA BREAD

Preparation Time: 10 minutes **Cooking Time:** 4 hours 10 minutes **Servings:** 7

INGREDIENTS

- Water, 1 cup
- Fresh spinach leaves (chopped), 1 cup
- Softened butter, 2 tsp
- Sugar, 1 tsp
- Bread flour, 3 cups
- Salt, 1 tsp
- Minced onion (instant), 2 tsp
- Instant yeast, 1 1/4 tsp
- Crumbled feta, 1 cup

DIRECTIONS

1. Add all ingredients, except spinach, cheese, and yeast, to the bread machine in the manufacturer's suggested order.
2. Add yeast to the yeast hopper. In the kneading cycle (last), add cheese and spinach.
3. Select the basic cycle with a light crust.

Nutritional Value: 190 kcal, Protein: 8g, Carbs: 26g, Fat: 6g
Note: Spinach Feta Bread is a savoury and flavourful bread filled with the goodness of fresh spinach and tangy feta cheese. It's perfect for serving with soups and salads or enjoyed on its own. Delight in the combination of spinach and feta in each slice.

9. RUM RAISIN BREAD

Preparation Time: 10 minutes **Cooking Time:** 3 hours 35 minutes **Servings:** 7

INGREDIENTS

- Dark rum, 2 tbsp
- Room temperature milk, 3/4 cup
- Salt, 1 tsp
- Packed brown sugar, 2 tbsp
- Egg, 1
- Bread flour, 2 1/4 cups
- Raisins, 1 cup
- Ground allspice, 1/2 tsp
- Bread machine yeast, 1 3/4 tsp
- Softened butter, 2 tbsp

DIRECTIONS

1. Place all ingredients into the pan of the bread machine, except raisins, according to the order suggested by the manufacturer.
2. Use the Sweet Cycle. At the ingredient signal, add raisins.
3. Serve fresh bread.

Nutritional Value: 180 kcal, Protein: 5g, Carbs: 34g, Fat: 3g
Note: Rum Raisin Bread is a sweet and aromatic bread with a delightful combination of rum-soaked raisins and warm spices. It's perfect for a special treat or enjoyed with your favourite spreads. Indulge in the rich flavours of rum and raisins in every slice.

10. BACON CORN BREAD

Preparation Time: 10 minutes **Cooking Time:** 2 hours 50 minutes **Servings:** 7

INGREDIENTS

- Oil, 2 tbsp
- Water, 1 1/3 cups
- Dry active yeast, 2 tsp
- Sugar, 1 1/2 tsp + 2 tbsp
- Bread flour, 4 cups
- Bacon (slices), 8
- Salt, 1 1/4 tsp
- Skim dry milk, 3 tbsp
- Cheddar cheese, 2 cups

DIRECTIONS

1. Add all ingredients, except bacon and cheese, to the bread machine in the manufacturer's suggested order.
2. Add bacon and cheese at the ingredient signal.
3. Select the basic cycle. Press start.

Nutritional Value: 190 kcal, Protein: 9g, Carbs: 29g, Fat: 5g
Note: Bacon Corn Bread is a savoury and indulgent bread that combines the smoky flavor of bacon with the richness of cheddar cheese. It's perfect for serving with soups or chili or enjoyed on its own. Savour the delicious combination of bacon and cheese in each bite.

11. OATMEAL COFFEE BREAD

Preparation Time: 10 minutes **Cooking Time:** 3 hours 10 minutes **Servings:** 7

INGREDIENTS

- Bread flour, 1 1/4 cups
- Cake flour, 1/2 cup + 2 tbsp
- Coffee powder, 1 1/2 tbsp
- Sugar, 2 tbsp + 1 tsp
- Water/milk, 1/2 cup + 2 tbsp
- Oats, 1/2 cup
- Butter, 1 tbsp + 1 tsp
- Milk powder, 3 tbsp + 2 tsp
- Yeast, 1 tsp

DIRECTIONS

1. Add all ingredients, except butter, to the bread machine in the suggested order by the manufacturer.
2. Select the basic cycle with a light crust. Add butter after the dough cycle.
3. Serve fresh bread.

Nutritional Value: 170 kcal, Protein: 6g, Carbs: 32g, Fat: 2g
Note: Oatmeal Coffee Bread is a hearty and comforting bread with the goodness of oats and the rich flavor of coffee. It's perfect for a warm breakfast or enjoyed with your favourite spreads. Experience the unique combination of oats and coffee in every slice.

12. CHERRY PISTACHIO BREAD

Preparation Time: 10 minutes   **Cooking Time:** 3 hours 10 minutes   **Servings:** 7

INGREDIENTS

- Egg, 1
- Cherry preserves, 1/2 cup
- Water, 1/2 cup
- Butter, 1/4 cup
- Salt, 1 tsp
- Active dry yeast, 2 1/4 tsp
- Almond extract, 1/2 tsp
- Chopped pistachios, 1/2 cup
- Bread flour, 3 1/2 cups

DIRECTIONS

1. Add all ingredients to the bread machine in the suggested order by the manufacturer.
2. Select the basic cycle. Press start. Check the dough; it should be a smooth ball. Add one tbsp of water or flour if too dry or too sticky, respectively.
3. Serve fresh bread.

Nutritional Value: 190 kcal, Protein: 6g, Carbs: 33g, Fat: 4g
Note: Cherry Pistachio Bread is a delightful and nutty bread with a burst of sweetness from cherry preserves and the crunch of pistachios. It's perfect for a special treat or enjoyed with afternoon tea. Indulge in the combination of cherries and pistachios in each slice.

13. BANANA COCONUT BREAD

Preparation Time: 10 minutes   **Cooking Time:** 3 hours 10 minutes   **Servings:** 7

INGREDIENTS

- Sugar, 8 tbsp
- Ripe bananas (large), 3
- Baking powder, 1 tsp
- Plain flour, 2 cups
- Salt, 1 tsp
- Coconut flakes, 1/2 cup
- Eggs, 2
- Vanilla, 1/2 tsp
- Cinnamon, 1/2 tsp

DIRECTIONS

1. Mix the sugar with mashed bananas.
2. Add all ingredients to the bread machine in the suggested order by the manufacturer.
3. Select the basic cycle. Press start.
4. Enjoy fresh bread.

Nutritional Value: 160 kcal, Protein: 3g, Carbs: 32g, Fat: 2g
Note: Banana Coconut Bread is a moist and tropical-flavoured bread that combines the sweetness of bananas with the delightful taste of coconut. It's perfect for breakfast or as a snack. Enjoy the tropical vibes and flavours in each slice.

14. EASY HONEY BEER BREAD

Preparation Time: 10 minutes **Cooking Time:** 1 hour 45 minutes **Servings:** 7

INGREDIENTS

- Olive oil, 2 tbsp
- Salt, 3/4 tsp
- Bread flour, 3 1/2 cups
- Fast-rising yeast, 1 3/4 tsp
- Flat beer, 1 1/8 cups
- Honey, 1/4 cup

DIRECTIONS

1. Add all ingredients to the bread machine in the suggested order by the manufacturer.
2. Select the basic cycle. Press start.
3. Enjoy fresh bread.

Nutritional Value: 180 kcal, Protein: 5g, Carbs: 33g, Fat: 2g
Note: Easy Honey Beer Bread is a simple and flavourful bread made with the richness of beer and the sweetness of honey. It's perfect for serving with soups, stews or enjoyed on its own. Savour the combination of beer and honey in every slice.

15. COFFEE MOLASSES BREAD

Preparation Time: 10 minutes **Cooking Time:** 2 hours 40 minutes **Servings:** 7

INGREDIENTS

- Honey, 3 tbsp
- Butter, 2 tbsp
- Salt, 1 1/2 tsp
- Bread flour, 3 cups
- Egg (whisked), 1
- Instant coffee (mixed in 1 cup of boiling water)
- Dark molasses, 1 tbsp
- Oats, 1/2 cup
- Yeast, 2 tsp

DIRECTIONS

1. Mix oats with one cup of boiling water and set it aside until it reaches 110°F or lukewarm temperature.
2. Add all ingredients to the bread machine in the suggested order by the manufacturer.
3. Select the basic cycle with a light crust setting. Press start.
4. Serve fresh bread.

Nutritional Value: 150 kcal, Protein: 5g, Carbs: 28g, Fat: 3g
Note: Coffee Molasses Bread is a unique and flavourful bread with the added richness of coffee and molasses. The oats give it a delightful texture.

16. CHERRY ALMOND BREAD

Preparation Time: 15 minutes **Cooking Time:** 1 hour 15 minutes **Servings:** 8

INGREDIENTS

- All-purpose flour, 2 cups
- Sugar, 3/4 cup
- Baking powder, 2 tsp
- Salt, 1/2 tsp
- Butter (melted), 1/4 cup
- Egg, 1
- Vanilla extract, 1 tsp
- Almond extract, 1/2 tsp
- Milk, 3/4 cup
- Fresh cherries (pitted and halved), 1 cup
- Sliced almonds, 1/2 cup

DIRECTIONS

1. Preheat the oven to 350°F (175°C) and grease a loaf pan.
2. In a large bowl, whisk together the flour, sugar, baking powder, and salt.
3. In a separate bowl, mix the melted butter, egg, vanilla extract, almond extract, and milk until well combined.
4. Pour the wet ingredients into the dry ingredients and stir until just combined. Fold in the cherries and sliced almonds.
5. Pour the batter into the prepared loaf pan and spread it evenly.
6. Bake for about 1 hour and 15 minutes, or until a toothpick inserted into the center comes out clean.
7. Remove from the oven and let it cool in the pan for 10 minutes. Then transfer to a wire rack to cool completely.
8. Slice and serve the cherry almond bread.

Nutritional Value: 180 kcal, Protein: 4g, Carbs: 29g, Fat: 6g
Note: Cherry Almond Bread is a delightful combination of sweet cherries and crunchy almonds. This moist and flavorful bread is perfect for breakfast or as a sweet treat with your afternoon tea. Enjoy its fruity and nutty goodness.

CHAPTER 4
GLOSSARY AND RESOURCES

5.1: GLOSSARY

- Proofing: also referred to as proving, is the ultimate rise of bread dough before heating. It refers to a specific pause within the more general fermentation process. During proofing, the dough's yeast continues germinating, releasing carbon dioxide gas and causing it to elevate. This phase enables the dough to acquire its final flavor and texture before being baked.
- Kneading: the process of incorporating gluten into the grain by kneading the dough. Gluten is a collection of proteins present in wheat, rye, and barley, among other grains. When the dough is kneaded, the gluten strands align and extend, forming a structure that captures the yeast's gas bubbles. This results in bread with a light and delicate texture.
- Crust: This term refers to the outer, tough surface of the bread. During baking, a series of chemical reactions known as the Maillard reaction gives the crust its characteristic brown colour and develop its flavor and texture. The crust safeguards the bread's delicate interior and provides a gratifying crunch when bitten.
- Crumb: This term describes the interior structure of a baguette of bread. A desirable crumb is light, delicate, and well-structured, with air pockets that are uniformly distributed. The crumb is the result of gluten development, the expansion of gas pockets during fermentation and proofing, and the bread's total hydration content.
- Gluten: is an assortment of proteins present in certain cereals, including wheat. It is responsible for bread dough's elasticity and chewiness. When flour is combined with water, gluten proteins form a network that provides structure to the dough. Gluten formation is essential in breadmaking because it helps capture gas produced by yeast, resulting in the bread's desired rise and texture.
- Yeast: a variety of fungi that ferments the carbohydrates in the dough to produce carbon dioxide and alcohol. Yeast is responsible for the bread dough's rise. In baking, there are two primary varieties of yeast: active dried yeast and instant yeast. Active dry yeast must be dissolved in tepid water prior to use, whereas instant yeast may be added directly to dried ingredients.
- Fermentation: is the process by which yeast consumes the carbohydrates in the dough to produce carbon dioxide and alcohol. Yeast converts carbohydrates into go during fermentation, resulting in the production of gas molecules that cause the dough to rise. As the yeast generates various compounds during fermentation, this process also contributes to the development of flavor in the bread.

- Baker's percentage: is a form of notation used in bread recipes in which the amount of each item is stated as a fraction of the flour's weight. This procedure provides a consistent and accurate technique for scaling up or down recipes. It also enables bakers to readily adjust the quantity of water, yeast, and other ingredients based on the intended bread characteristics.
- Scoring: is the process of creating shallow incisions on the surface of dough just before baking. This technique serves several purposes. It permits the departure of gases during baking, preventing the bread from exploding in random locations. Scoring also controls the expansion direction of the bread, resulting in a more uniform rise and an aesthetically pleasing loaf. The bread can be carved in a variety of patterns, giving it an artistic appearance.
- Artisan Bread: Artisan bread is the bread that is made in small quantities by expert bakers, as opposed to being mass-produced. It is frequently distinguished by its crusted exterior, open and expansive interior, and rich, complex flavours. Artisan bread is typically Preparationared using traditional techniques and premium ingredients, with a focus on craftsmanship and meticulousness.
- Sourdough: a variety of bread Preparationared with a naturally fermented dough containing microorganisms and wild yeast. It is renowned for its distinct sour taste and spongy consistency. The starter for sourdough bread is a grouping of flour and water that has been caused over time. The unique characteristics of sourdough bread are a result of the natural fermentation process, which often necessitates lengthier proofing times than bread Preparationared with commercial yeast.
- Bulk Fermentation: Bulk fermentation is a period of repose following the initial blending of dough, during which the yeast ferments and develops flavor. During this phase, the dough is allowed to rise in a lidded receptacle or container. Bulk fermentation is essential for gluten development and carbon dioxide creation, which contribute to the bread's rise and structure.
- Autolyze: this is a breadmaking technique in which flour and water are combined and permitted to settle prior to the addition of yeast and salt. This period of rest enables the flour to thoroughly absorb water and the gluten to begin developing, resulting in a dough that is more extensible and easier to work with. Autolyze can enhance the final bread's texture and flavor.
- Preferment: a portion of dough that has been Preparationared in advance and fermented before being incorporated into the final dough. Typically, it is Preparationared with flour, water, and a small quantity of yeast or sourdough starter. Preferences improve the flavor and texture of bread by extending the fermentation period and fostering the development of nuanced flavours.
- Banneton: Also known as a proofing basket, a banneton is a container or receptacle used for shaping and proofing bread dough. Typical banneton materials include cane or rattan, which enable the dough to breathe and create a gorgeous pattern on the bread's surface. The shape of the container supports the dough during proofing and imparts the bread's signature spiral pattern.

These terms and ideas are crucial to comprehend the art and science of bread making. You will gain a concentrated gain of the processes involved and be better equipped to experiment and create your own delectable bread if you become familiar with them.

5.2: RESOURCES

Consider the following additional reading and learning resources:

- Websites such as King Arthur Flour, Serious Eats, The Fresh Loaf, and Bread Magazine offer an abundance of culinary information, including detailed guides, tutorials, and discussion forums.
- Online classes: Websites such as Masterclass, Udemy, and Skill Share offer courses in bread making taught by professional bakers with hands-on demonstrations and guidance to improve your skills.

Remember that baking bread is a never-ending process of discovery and experimentation. Continuously expanding your knowledge and refining your skills will result in bread creations that are even more gratifying and delectable. Enjoy the culinary procedure, and good luck.

CONCLUSION

You have now acquired the skills and knowledge needed to confidently create delicious homemade bread using a bread machine. It doesn't matter if you are a novice or an expert bread maker; this book has provided you with a complete guide to mastering the art of bread making.

Throughout this journey, you have learned the essentials of bread machines, from understanding their functionality to choosing the right one for your needs. You have gained valuable insights into accurately measuring ingredients, programming the machine for different bread cycles, and troubleshooting general problems that might surface during the baking process.

From classic favourites to unique creations, you have experienced the joy of baking a variety of loaves of bread that suit different tastes, preferences, and dietary needs. The step-by-step instructions, detailed ingredient lists, and nutritional values have provided you with all the information necessary to create mouth-watering loaves of bread with confidence and success.

As you have discovered throughout this book, baking bread using a bread machine is not only convenient but also a rewarding and enjoyable experience. The aroma that fills your home as the bread bakes and the satisfaction of slicing it into a freshly baked loaf is truly special. By using a bread machine, you have unlocked the potential to create bread that rivals that of professional bakers right in the comfort of your own kitchen.

Remember, the journey doesn't end here. Continue to explore, experiment, and adapt the recipes to suit your preferences. Share your creations with loved ones and savour the joy that comes from sharing homemade bread made with care and passion.

Thank you for joining us on this breadmaking adventure. We hope The Easy Bread Machine Cookbook has inspired you to continue exploring the wonderful world of bread making. May your bread always rise, your flavours be rich, and your baking endeavours bring you endless satisfaction. Happy baking.

Thank you from the bottom of my heart for choosing to read this book!

It is with immense gratitude that I address these words to you. It gives me enormous pleasure to know that you have decided to give your time and attention to these pages that I have written with commitment and dedication.

Creating this book has been an exciting journey, and my hope is that you have found it as enjoyable and inspiring to read as I have in writing it. Every word was carefully chosen with the goal of conveying a message, a story or a new perspective to you.

I am aware that you have a multitude of choices available to you when it comes to books, and the fact that you chose mine is a source of great pride and happiness. Your choice is invaluable to me, as it is the support and interest of readers like you that give meaning to my work as a writer.

If you have enjoyed the journey you have taken with these pages, I kindly ask you to **share your experience with others**. Reader reviews are a vital tool for raising awareness of a book and helping other readers make an informed choice.

If you feel inspired to do so, you might **take a few minutes to write a positive review** in which you could share your opinions. Even a few words can make a huge difference and help introduce the book to a wider audience.

INDEX OF RECIPES

A

Almond Flour Bread: 59
Almond Flour Yeast Bread: 57
Almond Milk Bread: 58
Amish Wheat Bread: 103
Apple Butter Bread: 109
Apple Cider Bread: 111
Apple Spice Bread: 76
Argentinian Rolls: 38

B

Bacon Corn Bread: 130
Banana Coconut Bread: 131
Banana Whole-Wheat Bread: 77
Barmbrack Bread: 108
Basic Low-Carb Bread: 57
Basic Sourdough Bread: 67
Black Bread: 110
Black Olive Bread: 74
Blueberry Oatmeal Bread: 79
Blue Cheese Onion Bread: 43
Bread Machine - Bacon Bread: 91
Bread Machine Brioche: 118
Bread Machine Garlic Basil Bread: 94
Bread Machine Herb & Parmesan Bread Recipe: 96
Bread Machine Lemon Bread Recipe: 92
Bread Machine Pizza Dough with Variations: 93
Bread of the Dead (Pan de Muertos): 100
British Hot Cross Buns: 104
Brown Rice Bread: 123
Brown Rice & Cranberry Bread: 123

C

Caraway Dill Bread: 99
Challah: 101
Cheddar Cheese Basil Bread: 41
Cheesy Chipotle Bread: 40
Cherry Almond Bread: 133

Cherry Pistachio Bread: 131
Chia Sesame Bread: 85
Chile Cheese Bacon Bread: 46
Chocolate Chip Peanut Butter Banana Bread: 106
Chocolate Oatmeal Banana Bread: 113
Chocolate Sour Cream Bread: 107
Christmas Fruit Bread: 120
Cocoa Bread: 35
Coffee Cake: 111
Coffee Molasses Bread: 132
Confetti Bread: 52
Corn Bread: 56
Cottage Cheese Bread (Simple): 46
Cracked Pepper Bread: 98
Cracked Wheat Bread: 83
Cranberry Pecan Sourdough: 72
Crusty French Bread: 29
Crusty Honey Bread: 109
Crusty Sourdough Bread: 71

D

Dark Chocolate Sourdough: 73
Dark Rye Bread: 33
Double Cheese Bread: 44
Double Coconut Bread: 84

E

Easy Honey Beer Bread: 132
Eggnog Bread: 115
English Muffin Bread: 34
Everyday White Bread: 27

F

Faux Sourdough Bread: 68
Feta Oregano Bread: 48
Fiji Sweet Potato Bread: 105
Flaxseed Bread: 58
Flaxseed Honey Bread: 85

Fragrant Orange Bread: 80
French Onion Bread: 54
Fresh Blueberry Bread: 79

G

Gluten-Free Hawaiian Loaf: 124
Gluten-Free Peasant Bread: 124
Gluten-Free White Bread: 122
Goat Cheese Bread: 48
Golden Butternut Squash Raisin Bread: 55
Golden Corn Bread: 34
Golden Raisin Bread: 33
Grandma's Christmas Bread: 36
Greek Easter Bread: 105
Greek loaf: 39

H

Half Hour Bread: 40
Ham & Cheese Bread: 127
Hawaiian Bread: 104
Healthy Bran Bread: 32
Herb Sourdough: 72
Homemade Slider Buns: 38
Honey Cake: 119
Honeyed Bulgur Bread: 84
Honey Granola Bread: 110
Honey Whole-Wheat Bread: 27
Hot Buttered Rum Bread: 122
Hot Red Pepper Bread: 54

I

Italian Alperito Bread: 61
Italian Herb Bread: 96
Italian Panettone: 99
Italian Parmesan Bread: 47
Italian Pop Bread: 100

J

Jalapeño Corn Bread: 42
Jewish Bread Machine Challah: 39
Julekake: 121

K

Keto Baguette: 62
Keto Brioche Bread: 62
Keto Focaccia: 64

L

Lemon-Lime Blueberry Bread: 76
Lemon Poppy Seed Bread: 126
Lemon Sourdough Bread: 69
Lovely Oatmeal Bread: 30

M

Macadamia Bread: 60
Market Seed Bread: 83
Mashed Potato Bread: 51
Mediterranean Bread: 61
Mexican Bread: 95
Mexican Sweet Bread: 101
Moist Oatmeal Apple Bread: 80
Molasses Wheat Bread: 28
Mozzarella-Herb Bread: 49
Multigrain Bread: 82
Multigrain Sourdough Bread: 68
Multigrain Special Bread: 98
Mustard Rye Bread: 127

N

Nana's Gingerbread: 117
Nectarine Cobbler Bread: 107
Nutty Wheat Bread: 88

O

Oat Bran Molasses Bread: 31
Oatmeal Coffee Bread: 130
Oatmeal Seed Bread: 87
Oatmeal-Sunflower Bread Recipe: 90
Oatmeal Zucchini Bread: 53
Olive Cheese Bread: 43
Orange Cranberry Bread: 77
Oregano Onion Focaccia: 63

P

Panettone Bread: 114
Peaches & Cream Bread: 78
Peanut Butter Bread: 86
Pecan Maple Bread: 117
Pepper Asiago Loaf: 94
Pepperoni Bread: 97
Pineapple Coconut Bread: 73
Plum Orange Bread: 78
Portuguese Corn Bread: 103
Portuguese Sweet Bread: 116
Potato Thyme Bread: 56
Pretty Borscht Bread: 52
Pumpernickel Bread: 30
Pumpkin Coconut Bread: 112

Q

Quinoa Oatmeal Bread: 89
Quinoa Whole Wheat Bread: 86

R

Raisin Bran Bread: 126

Raisin & Nut Paska: 119
Raisin Seed Bread: 89
Rich Cheddar Bread: 47
Roasted Garlic Asiago Bread: 41
Roasted Garlic Bread for the Bread Machine: 93
Robust Date Bread: 75
Ron's Bread Machine White: 37
Rum Raisin Bread: 129
Russian Black Bread: 102
Russian Rye Bread: 102

S

Salami & Mozzarella Bread: 44
Sandwich Bread: 59
San Francisco Sourdough Bread: 70
Sauerkraut Rye Bread: 50
Sausage Herb Bread: 128
Savoury Onion Bread: 50
Simple Sourdough Starter (No-Yeast Whole Wheat Sourdough Starter): 66
Soft Egg Bread: 32
Sour Cream Maple Bread: 108
Sourdough Beer Bread: 70
Sourdough Cheddar Bread: 71
Sourdough Milk Bread: 69
Spaghetti Bread: 97
Spiced Raisin Bread: 95
Spiked Eggnog Bread: 121
Spinach Feta Bread: 129
Stollen Bread: 120
Strawberry Shortcake Bread: 81
Sunflower Bread: 88
Sweet Potato Bread: 55

T

Toasted Hazelnut Bread: 87
Toasted Pecan Bread: 82
Toasting Bread: 60
Tomato Herb Bread: 51
Traditional Italian Bread: 35
Traditional Pascha: 118
Triple Chocolate Bread: 113

V

Vanilla Almond Milk Bread: 112
Vegan Gluten-Free Bread: 125

W

Warm Spiced Pumpkin Bread: 75
White Bread: 36
White Bread II: 37
White Chocolate Cranberry Bread: 115
Whole-Wheat Bread: 28
Whole-Wheat Buttermilk Bread: 31
Whole-Wheat Challah: 116
Whole-Wheat Seed Bread: 81
Whole-Wheat Sourdough Bread: 67
Wild Rice Hazelnut Bread: 128

Y

Yeasted Carrot Bread: 49
Yeasted Pumpkin Bread: 53

Z

Za'atar Bread: 106
Zucchini Ciabatta: 64
Zucchini Pecan Bread: 125

Printed in Great Britain
by Amazon